Some JTT

1) Koala-fucki

2) Douche-swilling snatch maggot

3) cock-juggling thundercunt

4) Pit-sniffing vagina squirrel

The Queen of Everything

Tips on Life, Love, Parenting and Peacocks

KC Meadows

To Janis:
Thanks for being part of
JTT Nation. All hail!
XOXO
-Queen JTT

JTT Enterprises
PO Box 211
Versailles KY 40383
jttnation@gmail.com
www.jttnation.com

Limits of Liability and Disclaimer of Warranty

The author and publisher shall not be liable for your misuse of this material. This book is strictly for informational and educational purposes.

Warning - Disclaimer

The purpose of this book is to educate and entertain. The author and/or publisher do not guarantee that anyone following these techniques, suggestions, tips, ideas, or strategies will become successful. The author and/or publisher shall have neither liability nor responsibility to anyone with respect to any loss or damage caused, or alleged to be caused, directly or indirectly by the information contained in this book.

ISBN: 978-0-692-50542-7

Acknowledgements & Dedication

I must give a special acknowledgement to my Tiplets, without whom my story would be incomplete.

To Rah-rah: my lovely, spirited mini-me. Thanks for making me a mom and for being an inspiration to others. If you believe it, you'll always achieve it.

To Velvet: my beautiful, intelligent old soul. You are a source of happiness and pride, a friend to everyone you meet, whether they have two legs or four.

To Rasslin: my silly, sporty man-child. You taught me that while you may not know what you've got till it's gone, you also do not know what you've been missing until it arrives.

To Squirrel Master: my younger son, my baby. You see and experience the world differently than I do and with your endless antics offer a sometimes stunning but always hilarious perspective on the world around us.

And of course a special "thank you" to my husband, Mr. Tip, who makes my dreams come true and always gives me a happy ending. Yeah, I meant that how it sounds.

This book is dedicated to my loyal JTT Nation. Without all of you, I'd STILL be just another goofy bitch with a tiara, a megaphone and a yearning for a flock of peacocks. Thank you for being my tribe.

Epic Shit You Need To Know

1. My name is Just The Tip or JTT. I also answer to "The Queen of Errydamnthing." I say "fuck" a lot. I actually say alltheswears and when I run out of regular swears I make up fun new ones like "koala-fucking swamp gash" or "douche-swilling snatch maggot."

2. I'm happily married to an oh-so-sexy cop named Mr. Tip who also says "fuck" a lot. His creative swearing vocab pretty much extends to "douche" and "asshole" because "fuck" is uttered approximately every other word.

3. We have four beautiful crotchfruit who are not supposed to say "fuck" at all. I absolutely do not condone them swearing unless it is in appropriate context. Most of my material comes from hilarious daily interactions with them.

4. If you decide to stick around, you'll see the letters "ZFG" bandied about often. It means Zero Fucks Given. Embrace that shit. Trust me on this one.

5. My family and I are owned by a stable full of equine asshats. From mini-donkeys to Rocky Mountain Saddle Horses we have a shitload of critters with four hooves who spend their days plotting ways to rip down fencing or become inseminated so they may bestow surprise blessings on us in the dead of winter. They are pretty cute most of the time, but referenced as "asshats" for a reason.

6. We also have two silver labradors--Macie and Rosa Barks, a passel of pussies and an African Grey parrot named Cisco (who says "shit" more than "fuck" but is familiar with alltheswears as well).

7. I provide the option to obtain relevant t-shirts (that I design based on popular themes here on The Tip) from time to time. Some popular offerings have been "JTT says ZFG" and "Peace, Love and ZFG," but Crazy Train, Rosa Barks and "Cancer is a Godless Whore" are also adorned by many loyal Tippers across this great JTT Nation. "Dear Cancer--Get F&cked" is our best-seller.

8. I make light of every day situations. Sometimes it's about the kids, sometimes it's about people I interact with on a daily basis. Usually

the manner in which I do so is offensive to SOMEONE out there. I have no problem with people being offended. What I DO have a problem with is the fucking WHINING about it. Read it, don't read it, I don't care, but if you want to complain then kindly go choke on a used tampon.

9. I really want a fucking peacock (or flock of them) to call my own. I am obsessed with all things peacocky.

I think that covers most everything.

Peace, love and ZFG!!

Contents

Lead Vehicle in the Homecoming Parade

I dropped Rah-rah at her basketball game earlier and ran to do a few errands with the boys. For some unexplained reason, the cops had all the fucking intersections blocked so I "took a shortcut" to reach my destination.

Unfortunately, that intersection was also blocked and I needed cat food. While I do respect police authority (especially the handcuff part), I could see no possible reason for this traffic delay (other than a power outage or some shit) so I eased up carefully and turned onto Main Street.

That's right, I was the lead vehicle in the goddamn Homecoming Parade. And I led that processional Like. A. Boss.

Rasslin' noticed all of the people standing on the sidewalks staring and smiling as we slowly crept by.

Him: “Mom? What's going on with all these people?”

Me: <realizing my mistake> “Um. I guess they heard The Queen was in town.”

Him: <staring at me as if I had lost my damn mind> “Seriously, Mom. Not EVERYONE knows you're the Queen. What's happening?"

I rolled down the windows. “Just wave,” I hissed. “Give the people what they want.”

He waved his ass off. And I drove my dirty ride until I had to turn again to get to the store, but those few intersections were motherfucking glorious. All hail, bitches.

Megaphone Chronicles: Day 1

We are on vacation and last night we were five floors above the Partay of the Century. A major sausage-fest was swinging below and it wasn't long before there was a knock at our door. It was a trashed frat boy with a megaphone and a humble (but very amplified) request for toilet paper. He said that he and his friends were on a scavenger hunt. I am 8000% sure that the ONLY thing on the fucking list was ASS, but finding that is impossible without a well-wiped butthole. I took pity and found him a half a roll then sent him (and his megaphone--I really tried to negotiate a trade) on his way.

Mr. Tip and I briefly discussed joining them in the hot tub, but I hadn't had enough to drink and there was no good reason to revisit my college days on a family vacay, so we went to bed like a couple of lame asses after watching Iron Man 3.

This morning, my Dad got up early to conduct some business via the phone. It was around 7 am and everyone was still sleeping, including a tiplet on the couch. After he'd concluded his call, he took a closer look at the sleeping form on the couch. It had a tattoo. A big one. It was not a tiplet. It was the fucking drunk megaphone frat guy.

He was passed out with his phone in one hand and megaphone in the other. Dad, thinking perhaps Mr. Tip had invited this poor, homeless partying soul to our couch in a moment of charitable brotherhood, came and nearly beat our bedroom door down. Mr. Tip, sleep riddled and confused, assured him that he had invited no one into our domain, (because I'm scared of vampires and shit) went into full blown cop mode, retrieved his pistol, and escorted our hungover guest out of our apartment then handed him his phone.

Nearly giddy with the excitement of it all, I dashed into the living area and saw the most wonderful thing: his abandoned megaphone. Seems he was willing to trade after all.

Tonight, I'm going on a scavenger hunt.

Megaphone Chronicles: Day 2

It is a lovely (albeit windy) night here on the gulf. After several heartfelt requests, Mr. Tip agreed to grill the hell out of some meat. A breeze ripped through the grilling area, fueled the fuck out of the charcoal and damn near caught my pretty-much-drunk ass on fire. Luckily I was able to scream into my megaphone and announce my close encounter to all of the guests in the vicinity. They are all glad I still have most of my eyebrows and no disfiguring burns. I heart my megaphone. It saved my life.

I love watching local news in locations I am not familiar with. Mostly, I enjoy getting to know the news anchors.

Local News: "Blah blah blah, and now, Erin Feces is on location with a story about school bullying."

Me: "Do you think that's just her professional name?"

My Mom: "I don't know. How the hell would I know?"

Me: "Well, how would someone get a freaking name like FEE-CEES??"

My Mom: <laughing> "I'm pretty sure it was Weasley."

Me: "No way. That's NOT what they said." <into my megaphone> "FECES IS A SHITTY NAME FOR A NEWS ANCHOR."

Now Mr. Tip has taken away my megaphone. While he finds me witty and hilarious, he does not seem to enjoy me 'amplified'. God damn, I hope someone with another cool toy crashes our pad tonight.

Sweet dreams, Tippers.

Megaphone Chronicles: Day 3

Our beach attendant (you know, the Jo-Jo that sets up my beach chairs, brings me drinks, worships the very sand I walk on) sucks a big, fat salty dick this year. I'm trying to decide if I'm just not his type (he's 4'2, I'm 6'), or if Mr. Tip telling him he's an asshole is the reason for his douchebaggery, but either way I hope he gets sand fleas.

Yesterday I flounced down to the beach with my cooler, iPad, a shitload of cookies and of course, my megaphone. He had my chairs set up on the SECOND ROW where I couldn't see a damn thing. I announced my displeasure over my megaphone.

Asshole lifeguard: "Where did you get that megaphone?"

Me: "From your mother."

Asshole lifeguard: <sternly> "Where. Did. You. Get. It."

Me: "From the drunk guy that ended up sleeping on my couch."

Asshole lifeguard: "I think it belongs in the guard shack."

Me: "Oh no, Bitch. Possession is 9/10ths of the law."

Asshole lifeguard: "Look on the handle. Does it say FWB?"

Me: "It's very faded..."

Asshole lifeguard: "Our loudspeaker went missing on Sunday."

Me: "Goddammit. I wish that bastard piece of shit was still here, I'd kick him in the nuts. See? YOU DON'T WANNA PISS ME OFF."

Asshole lifeguard: <holding out his hand> "Can I have it back?"

Me: <choking back tears> "Will you love it as much as I have? AND will you give me a front row seat for the rest of the week?"

Asshole lifeguard: <rolling his eyes> "Whatever."

So today, my crushed spirit is off in search of a megaphone and this entire motherfucking inhabited stretch of coast has NO MOTHERFUCKING MEGAPHONES and I miss mine SO BAD.

Megaphone Chronicles: Day 4

I bought a megaphone. Mr. Tip was pissed (because it was a hundred dollars for some shit we don't NEED. He wishes I'd never seen the megaphone in the first place. I give zero fucks. He got ugly boots and while I made FUN of him, I did not say they were NOT NECESSARY...) but the bottom line is I now have my OWN FUCKING MEGAPHONE that says Property Of JTT. Suck on that, Asshole Lifeguard.

And omg it's epic. It has a siren and everything. Also, I met a Tipper today. In freaking real life. I think she was disappointed that I didn't drool or shit myself. She also got to meet the formerly Broken Tip who was kind enough to show her leg scar, then do a bunch of cheer splits/jumps in the middle of the store after I gave her money to buy a smoothie and she got Starbucks instead and lost her freaking mind on a major sugar/caffeine buzz.

I am abso-fucking-loutely blown away by the fact that I found someone I heart through my ridiculous ramblings here on the Tip. Someone I never would have met otherwise. So we're getting together again to take pictures, grill out, introduce our kids, etc. I might even let her hold my megaphone. She's THAT badass.

Peace and love, Tippers <3

Megaphone Chronicles: Day 5

Note: Making sex noises on the balcony at sunrise ON THE MEGAPHONE is a fine way to start any day, especially a Thursday. Mr. Tip missed some of my best work because he was sleeping. Poor Mr. Tip...

After sharing my morning itinerary via megaphone, Mr. Tip pointed out that I forgot to add "Do some research," to my list.

"What am I supposed to be researching?" I trumpeted (then added a siren because it seemed like an appropriate time to make use of that awesome feature).

"How about 'How to remove a megaphone from your colon'," he mumbled.

"Me and my megaphone (and colon) are going to the beach. Where we are fucking appreciated."

I just noticed my daughter having a discussion on the beach with a boy close to her age. My megaphone came in mighty fucking handy. "SIR, STEP AWAY FROM THE GIRL." Now he's gone and she's horrified, but I pointed out that any potential future boyfriend will have to put up with my shit anyway. Might as well help her cull em out of the gate.

In other news, the toddler sitting next to me is eating handfuls of sand, unchecked.

Megaphone: "THAT WILL BE AN AWESOME DIAPER."

Megaphone Chronicles: Day 6

Me: "I'm ready to go to the beach."

7-year old: "Don't forget your megaphone, Mom!"

Mr. Tip: <sarcastically> "Maybe if we are lucky, she'll bring the camera too."

Me: <grabbing the camera> "Shit I almost forgot!"

So we're chillin' on the beach and my daughter starts snapping pictures of all kinds of things, kites, birds, bird shit, my megaphone, Mr. Tip's beer, her sister sulking under the umbrella...when Mr. Tip offered to take our picture. She gave him the camera, then we posed prettily in the surf.

He took about 50 fucking shots. One blurry one of the pair of us, and 49 fairly clear ones of my tits.

I'm sure he will treasure those for years to come.

Megaphone Chronicles: Day 7

The Tips are soaking up these last few moments on the beach before heading home. “Meg” is already packed away in the truck. When I protested, (bitch wanted to ride shotgun with ME) Mr. Tip assured me she would be happier in the back--she needs a vacation, too. Dammit, I miss her. It's very quiet and peaceful now. I hate that shit. XOXO.

I just accidentally shook my boob out of my bikini top in an effort to shake water out of my ear. Without the aid of a megaphone, my daughters announced this fact to the entire population of beach goers.

Tip of the Day: When exposed tits are involved, you don't need a megaphone to get people's attention.

And I still have fucking water in my ear.

Lost Towels

One afternoon I realized we were missing a few beach towels. Building security had warned us several times against hanging our shit off the balcony but my Zero Fucks Given policy overruled their No Towels Flapping one. I figured they had fallen off, so 12-year old Tiplet, Meg and I went off in search of them.

We couldn't locate any personnel (even though the siren was in full effect) but finally obtained the attention of a Hispanic groundskeeper.

"Where is the lost and found?" I asked, without amplification.

He shrugged and smiled. I assumed he failed to hear me. "I LOST MY TOWELS," I trumpeted. "WHERE MIGHT THEY BE??"

He laughed. "No habla englais!"

My bad. Let me try this another way: "WHERE-O ARE MY TOWEL-OS?" Then I removed my wrap from my waist and made some fluttering motions to mime them falling off the balcony. My 12-year old rolled her eyes, and said "Mom? I don't think he understands but he can HEAR you fine."

I never found my fucking towels. I totally rocked the Espanol, but I think my attempt at charades was an epic fail. He handed me two bucks.

Yeah. Pretty sure he thought I was giving him a strip tease.

Additional Megaphone Uses

Meg and I are helping Mr. Tip watch football by repeating shit he says like

"THAT'S FUCKING HOLDING" or

"WHAT THE HELL ARE YOU THINKING YOU STUPID SHITTARD?" or

"OH MY GAWD He DROPPED the GODDAMN BALL."

And we're also making some other fucking things up that don't have much to do with football like "I WANT ANOTHER BISCUIT WITH JELLY!" and "THEY CALLED SCHOOL OFF FOR TOMORROW." and "IS WINTER BREAK EVER GOING TO END? PLEASE. TINY BABY JESUS. HAVE MERCY."

Helluva game. Boom.

Love Story: My side

I was 19 and home from college on summer vacation. Mr. Tip had just been hired on the local police force. We both grew up in the same small town, but he is eight years older than me so we never actually knew each other.

The fair was in town. The county fair is a HUGE deal in our community because every single person turns up for it--it's a reunion with cotton candy, fair rides, horse shows and barkers. I happened to be off work so my mother told me to get my shit together because we were heading out for the night.

My sister was only 10 years old at the time and my brother was running in a cross country match so my parents reasoned that I could let my sis tag along with me whilst I made my reunion rounds. It ended up raining. As in completely PISSING rain. It was raining so hard I took my shoes off and slogged through the mud. Everyone had gone home and I was standing off to the side waiting for my brother to get done and watching my sister ride the gdamn carousel for the 20th time. (This was before ipods and shit, so kids back then were easily amused.)

About that time a female deputy walked up to me and asked how old I was. I froze in horror. WTF did she THINK I had done? I was with my PARENTS for chrissakes, I was being a REALLY GOOD girl. I was like "Um, I'm 19, why?" And she said "Well, one of our new guys saw you walking around and he thinks you're cute and I thought it would be FUNNY if you came over and said hello, but I wanted to make sure you were legal."

Oh, well. Thank you so much for the heart attack. I was TOTALLY bored with the babysitting gig and the cross country stuff was wrapping up so I sent my sis back to my parents and followed this lady back up to the Officer's Tent. Primarily because it was raining...there was NO WAY I had any interest in ruining my college fun by dating a freaking cop. My dad knew most of the guys on the force anyway…and that's like the eleventh commandment: Thou shalt not get involved with anyone your father is buddies with.

I stepped under the awning, and Mr. Tip turned around. He kind of rolled his eyes at the woman who'd been busily playing matchmaker and smiled at me. And for a second, my heart stopped in my chest. He had the most gorgeous blue eyes and was a fucking STUD in his uniform. We talked for awhile, decided we had a few things in common and he said he'd give me a call sometime.

The next day I was eating cereal in the kitchen when my mom yelled "THE COPS ARE HERE! Where the hell is your brother?" I was quick to assure her that it was probably my new po-po friend. The color drained from her face and she said "OMG, you were FLIRTING in the POLICE TENT last night?" Yes, Mother. Yes I was. "I thought you were just in there staying DRY!"

Mr. Tip came in, said hello, walked with me up to the barn to meet my horses then announced that he needed to use the restroom. I was thinking he should just take a piss outside like a real country boy, but he went into the bathroom and proceeded to take the most ungodly shit I've ever heard/smelled. I guess he was nervous. My mom and I were in tears from the laughing.

After he'd totally cleansed his colon, Mr. Tip sauntered back into the living room and announced he'd best be getting back to town. It was epic.

The next night I had planned to see him out at the fair again. I was less than enchanted after the shitting up the toilet incident, but I was going to town with a few of my girlfriends anyway. I figured I would go with them, wait til he got off work and he could take me home. Alcohol might have been involved.

I was kind of wandering around looking for him when I saw a HAWT guy in jeans and a cowboy hat sauntering down from the show barn. I turned to my friend and said "To hell with cops, I'm gonna get me a COWBOY!" and stumbled off in his general direction. When the distance between us was approximately half, he turned, saw me and smiled--and I realized it was Mr. Tip. He'd taken the night off so we could hang out. I giggled and said "I think I want to marry you." The rest? Is history. A beautiful, tumultuous, amazing history that has made us who we are today. I'm thankful for every second :)

The Meeting: Mr. Tip's Story

As I understand it, I am under some pressure to give MY side of the most glorious event in the history of my life--The Night JTT and I Became Acquainted. All of the fair stuff is completely accurate: A fellow officer and I were on foot patrol--trolling the midway, having the typical young and single rookie cop type of conversation:

"Would you?"

"Hell yeah, are you kidding me?"

"How about her?"

"Hell no, not even with your dick" ...etc.

I know, it makes me sound like a complete douchebag asshole, but I was young and in uniform and newly exposed to the powers of my position. After several passes weeding out the hotties and lot lizards I thought we'd picked through most of them when I saw a vision.

She was tall and blonde, wearing jeans right out of a country song, a white tee shirt and boots. I caught up to my fellow officer and pointed her out. He agreed that she was completely fuckable, but did not know the story behind that fine creation so we assumed she was from out of town.

Casually I approached one of the female officers who had been asking about the kind of girl I'd go for earlier that week, and went out of my way to drag her around the fair until we found JTT again. I'll never forget the words I said: "Now THAT'S the kind of girl I'd like to meet. She's pretty, she's country, she's not all dolled up and she's not here to impress anyone."

So my fellow officer went into full blown detective mode. It started raining and I was hungry so I grabbed a pork sandwich and hunkered down in the Officer's Tent. I had a mouthful of barbecue but turned around just in time to see my cohort arrive in the shelter with a soaking JTT. I thought she was hot when she was dry, but drenched and dripping was an even better look on her. I almost choked on my sandwich, but managed to grin and shake her hand.

We literally talked for hours in the rain under the tent. I think all my swag was gone by then and I gave her ten ways to get in touch with me. My super cool beeper number, my cell, my home phone, my office, my parents' phone, etc. because I wanted to be sure she knew I was available if she wanted to chat. I couldn't WAIT to give her a ride in my cruiser.

An amusing side note: At one point in the evening JTT's mom was close by having a conversation with an officer she knew and she jokingly commented that she had dragged JTT to the fair to find her a husband. We still have a good laugh about that one.

The next day I decided I'd be REALLY cool and cruise by and see JTT at her house. It was a scene straight out of a movie. I really should set things up by letting you know that lunch is a fantastic daily event where all the guys get together in the squad room and eat as much greasy, nasty bullshit as they can stuff down. Most of our local fast food restaurants offer free meals to guys in uniform, and THAT day we'd enjoyed a SHITLOAD of questionable burritos.

As I entered the home of my unknown future wife (whom I thought to be drop dead gorgeous already) I found her eating cereal and chatting with her mother who was hanging wallpaper in the hallway. A few pleasantries were exchanged and I was oozing coolness with my uniform and authority and all.

JTT flounced up to the barn munching on her Lucky Charms with me in tow and showed me her stable and equine asshats and invited me to come riding with her sometime. I was just realizing that I was REALLY into this girl when I had the most gawd awful cramps erupt in my stomach.

All I could think was "holy shit, what am I going to do?" Normally there would be time for a fake call and a lights-and-siren run to the station or a secret dumping hole, but this one came out of nowhere and there was no time to wait. It was here. It was now.

I don't know if any of you have ever had to use every ounce of power to clinch your ass cheeks together to keep from shitting on yourself, but it can reduce the coolest, strongest man to tears. The walk to the bathroom was a feat in and of itself. Permission to use the bathroom was granted, and wouldn't you know it...the toilet is not around the corner, not down the hall, not in the fucking basement...it is literally TWO FUCKING FEET AWAY from where my future Mother-in-law and her stunningly gorgeous daughter (whom I want to get to know better) are HANGING WALLPAPER in the FUCKING HALLWAY.

I clinch and pretend not to clinch and sidle into the bathroom. It's difficult to come out of a gun belt when you've got time, but when shit is on the verge of flying out of your ass...well, I was ripping off belt keepers and undoing buckles and straps and praying to TinyBabyJesus that I could just get my ass somewhere NEAR the toilet when finally the belt came loose and hit the ground with a thud.

I was in complete Panic Mode and thought "I'll just turn the fan on and let a little out at a time!" But when I hit the switch, there was silence. THE GODDAMN MOTHERFUCKING PIECE OF SHIT FAN DIDN'T WORK. At this point, I there was no more shame in my game. I gave it up and just let it happen.

It was like pouring a bucket of gravel in a baby pool and it smelled like a overused port-a-john on a hot summer's day. I started sweating like a whore in church, swearing quietly under my breath, praying for the damn toilet to swallow me up.

Eventually it was over. I gathered what was left of my self respect and dignity and marched out of the bathroom to red faces and smiles. I politely excused myself, having left my mark and my lasting memory. I know it had to take hours for the stink to fade. What a fan-fucking-tastic first impression. I guess it worked though, because she DID go out with me, we fell in love and I am a LUCKY, LUCKY guy.

Mothballs

When Mr. Tip and I first got married, we lived in a shithole that had fucking skunks living underneath it so we used mothballs to ward them off. Which translates to I smelled a lot of skunk MIXED with mothballs and pretty much hated life.

We are past the point of skunks in our crawlspace now, but the smell of mothballs still gives me a bit of a panic attack.

A few days ago we were at a store we don't often frequent and I caught a whiff.

Me: "Ew, gross."

Rassslin: <snurling his nose> "What's that SMELL?"

Me: "I think it's mothballs."

Rasslin: "Are they big?"

Me: <making a dime sized circle with my hand> "I guess they're about this big, but let's go. It's nasty."

Rasslin: <digesting this information> "Well is that why it's so hard for them to FLY?"

Me: "WTF are you TALKING ABOUT?"

Rasslin: "The boy moths. Do they fly all slow because their balls are SO BIG?"

Velvet: <knowledgeably> "I don't know how moths get around, but butterflies float gently so they are all girls I think."

Holy shit. This is totally outside of the realm of my ability to craft a smart-assed/clever response. So I said what any good mother would: "Yeah, I guess..."

Shit Balls

Our kids were invited to a birthday party at one of those huge indoor playground type places--you know, the kind that you need two valiums and a bottle of wine before even thinking of going in? Welp, I arrived sans tranquilizers and alcohol, so after three minutes I was desperately searching for something with which to slit my wrists.

My children immediately scattered. I found a place fairly close to the door so I could monitor their whereabouts and be mostly certain they were not accompanying random child molesters into the parking lot. I was just getting comfy when a lady came up and asked, "Does anyone have an extra shirt?"

My sarcastic inclination was to assure her that I did indeed keep extra shirts in all sizes and colors with me at all times, but I was curious. "Who needs an extra shirt?"

"Oh, my son," she said, almost apologetically. "Someone pooped in the balls."

Hold the fucking phone. You mean to tell me someone took a SHIT in the ball pit?? Excuse me while my nightmare is realized.

I didn't wait to hear the rest of the shitty shirt story, but I did get to the ball pit in time to see my 6-year old Squirrel Master dive in face first. It was goddamn glorious. "MOM LOOK! I'M IN THE BALLS!!!" he exalted, shitty rubber balls raining all around him in an explosion of awesome.

If you need me, I'll be over here in the corner, eating cake and drinking wine in preparation for the imminent Norovirus outbreak. Oh well, I can stand to lose a few pounds. I'm one good flu away from my size 6s.

Spare Panties

I've been striving to improve my preparedness and organization skills. Recently, I accidentally showed my ass in a public venue. Eager to reduce my odds of a reoccurrence, I asked my younger daughter to put a pair of my underwear in my pool bag.

"What kind should I get?" she asked.

I have three grades of panties. Grade III--Time of The Month drawers. These bitches have one foot in the grave, holes, stains, loose elastic etc. Grade II--Cute but Functional. A self-explanatory category. Grade 1--Date Night Hootchies. These have a distinct allotted wear time and place-maybe ten minutes and on the floor.

"Just get some decent ones. I don't really care. Something that covers my ass please."

Later, I was ready to change into my underwear after swimming, and asked my daughter where she'd stuck my drawers. "They aren't in the pool bag? I guess I forgot them. Sorry." Fucking awesome.

Because I was somewhat scarred from my last commando performance, I elected to wear my wet bathing suit under my damn blue jeans. I made a mental note to grab a pair when I got home. Then I forgot about it. Of course I forgot about it.

A few days later I was sitting with my optician, having my new glasses fitted. He wanted my insurance card. "Please hand me my wallet," I instructed my son.

Two seconds later he exclaims, "OH LOOK MOM! I found your thongs!" and pulled out arguably the raunchiest pair in my arsenal.

"OHMYGAWD," snapped my eldest. "She said she wanted GRUNGY underwear, NOT sexy ones."

And NOT stuffed in my fucking purse to be whipped out in front of a bunch of old ladies (peering judgmentally through their bifocals) like a rabbit out of a magician's hat.

The look on the guy fitting my shit was PRICELESS, though. I just shrugged and said "Yup, that's how I roll. Always keep a spare."

"Yeah," he stammered. "That's um, something my mom always recommended."

She taught you right.

Epic.

Nuts

I have become obsessed with these cool little Breakfast To Go packets. They have around 100 calories and they're quite filling. But if I'm being honest, the real reason I love them is because they're composed primarily of nuts, (which I actually enjoy) and also the WORD 'nuts' (definitely one of my favorites).

Mr. Tip and I have devised a game featuring these 'nut sacks' (if you will). The object of the game is to say the word 'nuts' in as many obscene ways as possible without actually saying anything obscene. For example: "Honey, you have some nut on your chin" is an acceptable phrase.

So is "Dear? Grab my nuts, I'm trying to drive."

Or my favorite, "These nuts are salty. But they taste amazing."

This game can last an extraordinary length of time. In fact, the only time we cannot play is when I don't have nuts, so I tend to keep a bag with me at all times (in case I get bored).

Earlier my 6-year old gasped, "OMG, MOMMY!!! Your NUTS are ABOUT to FALL OUT of your PANTS! Put them up before everyone sees them!"

Loudly, in a crowd.

The Bag Of Nuts

It doesn't happen often, but OCCASIONALLY, I enjoy a good, old-fashioned personal challenge. My self-issued dare today is to work the phrase "bag of nuts" into any conversation I have. I already scored at the feed store, and a nutbag discussion with my doctor is everyday fare. My optometrist has already seen my fucking underwear, so he should be easy. The mailman has seen my boobs...again, barely a blip on the radar. The only one I'm worried about is the teacher-conference I have scheduled this afternoon. Peace, love and ZFG :)

Awkward convo with the optometrist:

Me: "I can't decide which frames I want."

Him: "Well, try some on."

Me: "Ok, just keep in mind that the look I'm going for is 'Naughty Librarian' not 'Nerdy Cougar'."

Him: <giggling a bit nervously> "So, I really like the Prada. Do you like the Prada?"

Me: "Does a hungry squirrel like a bag of nuts? Yeah I like the Prada, but I also like being able to buy groceries."

Him: "Hah! Well, we are running a special blah, blah, blah..." <then he said a bunch of shit about the special whilst I weighed the pros and cons of the Coach vs Ralph vs Prada...I am not the best decision maker>

Random Old Lady Wearing a Pair of Prada: "I LOVE my Prada."

Bitch please. You just fucking boomed my point. Now go away.

Me: <imploring the optometrist over the top of the Coach frames> "Seriously. Librarian, not Cougar."

Him: "Put your hair up."

Finally. He freaking GETS me!!! And it's Coach for the win.

It is quite difficult to work 'bag of nuts' seamlessly into an order at Chick-fil-a. I finally went with “Do you all still carry those little bags of nuts to put on salads?” They do not. Judging from the confusion on her face, they never did.

ZFG.

Still a win.

Pharmacy Nuts

To the pharmacist who got a little testy (HAHA SEE WHAT I DID?):

Him: "They just called in ONE script and I got it a few minutes ago."

Me: "Fine. When should I plan on picking it up?"

Him: <rolling his eyes slightly> "At least an hour."

Me: "Cool. I'm not in a major hurry. No need to get your bag of nuts in a wad..."

Him: <silence, slack jawed staring> "Ummmmm..."

Me: <to Mr. Tip> "Oh god. I took it too far. He's having a coronary."

Mr. Tip: <guiding me out> "Yup. You're done."

Fuck that.

Now I'm COMMITTED.

Shit just got real.

Educated Nuts

Given the somewhat traumatic nature of the pharmacy exchange, I pussed out a bit on the teacher conference.

Teacher: "Your daughter is doing very well in my class. She works hard and commits herself completely to any project I assign."

Me: "Good!" <considering> "I think she gets that from me."

Teacher: "Haha!"

Me: "Ok, great talk. Thanks for meeting with me. I'm going to run some errands and I'll be back to pick her up. Do you know where she is? I brought her a bag of nuts to snack on."

Teacher: "She'll be here soon, do you want to leave them with me? I'll make sure she gets them!"

No dammit. I don't actually have any nut bags. But I'm muthafuckin' COMMITTED to a PROJECT.

But I said: "That's okay, I'll find her on my way out."

Now poor nutless Rah-rah is going to wonder what the hell happened to her snack. ZFG. Stand back, I'm on a mission.

Mr. Tip was scared of my level of commitment to Project: Bag of Nuts, so instead of taking me to wrestling practice, (which would have been a glorious wrap-up) he dropped me off at home. And when I say 'dropped me off at home', I mean he drove fucking 34 miles out of his way to prohibit any nut bag discussions with wrestlers, their parents and/or coaches. I'm cool with that. All day win, Tippers.

Spare Panties

My Rah-rah had cheer practice this morning, and despite a somewhat ominous sky, I took the kids to the pool while we waited for her. I understand that some people make an effort to look presentable in public.

But as the current resident Giver Of Zero Fucks, that person was not me today. I threw on an old pair of sweats and a tank top over my bathing suit and went on my merry way.

The pool was great. Not too crowded, no one was being instructed to piss in it, and there was a perfect mix of sun and clouds.

My Squirrel Master begged me to go in with him. I agreed. I was sweating a little after all. We paddled around until I realized that it was almost time to pick my kid up from practice. I hadn't really thought shit through when I got in the water because I had failed to bring an alternate set of undergarments and did NOT have enough time to dry out.

This might be a problem for Fuck Givers, but JTT is kind of a rockstar. While I was not willing to forego breast support (wet boobies never hurt anyone) there was not a chance in hell I was going to look like I pissed my sweats.

So I went commando. Duh.

I emerged from the bath house feeling refreshed and free. My children had followed instructions and had all of our items packed up to go. They met me near the exit, close to the concession stand. Which is where my 6-year old threw a massive junebug at Rasslin (who is terrified of all of the bugs). His blood-curdling scream commanded the attention of most of the patrons, so everyone was staring when he ripped down my fucking pants in a frantic effort to save himself. I have officially shown more skin at our local watering hole than Thong Lady and Fat Speedo Man combined. And I now understand the importance of underwear.

Football Uniform

Football conditioning is still going strong. While the kids have started wearing their helmets at practice, they won't go full gear for another week or two...so it's a sea of boys in mismatched athletic shorts and t-shirts.

When we got home tonight, I told my kids to go wash their dirty asses in the shower. In a rare display of obedience, Rasslin began to strip down (in the middle of the living room). Despite the fact that they're doing drills and bear crawls and up/downs and burpees and shit, my son had elected to forego his underwear.

Me: "OMG. Where the hell are your underwear?"

Him: "Um. In my drawer I guess."

Me: "You didn't wear any to practice???"

Him: "Nope."

Me: "What the FRICK were you thinking?"

Him: "You said it was time to go and I didn't have time to put some on. I was thinking that I didn't want you to yell at me. And also I was thinking that sometimes it's good to air out your junk."

Me: <shaking my head> "Could you PLEASE wear underwear from now on? Your junk should NOT be free whilst playing contact sports. Besides, no one wants to see your ass in the event your pants are ripped down without warning."

Him: <giggling> "Yeah. You're one to talk, Mom."

The Amazing Race

Mr. Tip and I have been married for more than fourteen years.

One of the reasons why we are still married is because we've learned things we can NOT do together as a couple. Luckily there are a few things we CAN do...but it's a delicate balance.

Things we do NOT do well together:

1. Play Monopoly (He is a Know-it-all asshole. And kind of a cheater.)

2. Take long road trips. (He is a Know-it all asshole who has to pee a lot and sucks at reading maps. And he doesn't like to talk about all of the things while he's driving. And he plays lots of 80s rock on the radio. Loud.)

3. Anything physically competitive. (He loves to win. I give zero fucks.)

Things we do well together:

1. Horseback riding. (It's my thing. I'm better at it than him which removes any air of competition and he looks awesome in his tight jeans and boots.)

2. Raise our children. (Neither one of us is afraid to dole out an ass-whoopin' when needed, but we both love em like crazy)

3. Have frequent, awesome sex. (Really, you can throw out all the other shit, if you've got that it's all good.)

ANYWAY, now that I've gotten back in shape, he wants me to do this Mud Run/Obstacle Course charity thing with him next month. I was all, Ummmmm...HELL no. He was all, "Why NOT? You can TOTALLY do ALL that stuff they have set up." And I was all, refer to #3. (On either list.)

It all comes down to this: He would fucking die before he would fail to complete an obstacle. I would fucking die if I broke a nail. Then he would yell at me (to motivate me or some other dumb, misguided shit) and I would scream something classy like "Yeah? How's about FUCK YOU," whilst stomping off/quitting/plotting revenge. It's just a bad plan.

Today, he had an even better idea. "OMG HONEY. WE SHOULD TOTALLY APPLY FOR 'THE AMAZING RACE'! You would kick ass at the mental puzzle things and the negotiating. I could do all the stupid physical shit like launch watermelons, carry a donkey around, milk a cat, wtf ever...it would be epic!" Rah-rah, listening intently, completely cracked up. "Dad! You all fight over which way is best to GET HOME. PLUS you'd both have to eat pig guts and stuff. Besides, what if Mom broke a nail or something? Did you think about that???"

Ex-fuckin-actly.

How ZFG was Born:

Most of you know that my husband is deeply involved in our local small-town youth football league. He is the head coach of our older son's 9-10 year old team. Primarily because I sleep with him, I earned the esteemed title of "Team Mom". I'm still not sure how this happened. (Last year I literally came within a twat-hair of a full blown cat fight with another parent. I probably would have lost--she has a good 200 lbs on me, but I would have gone down swinging. Bitch.)

Tonight we were doing a youth player intro at the high school scrimmage, and everyone was in their league issued t-shirts. There were crotchfruit everywhere (dressed identically) and 100 parents asking me shit I didn't know answers to. And it was PISSING rain.

After a particularly annoying encounter with one individual, I muttered "And you are welcome to go fuck yourself" under my breath as she meandered off (the invitation was uncharacteristically quiet...it's early in the season and I'm pacing myself). Just then another age division's Team Mom came up and said "Why didn't you wear your t-shirt?"

"I didn't GET a t-shirt," I explained.

"You really NEED a t-shirt so people know you're involved," she insisted. "I got one. Do you want one?"

"Seriously?" I questioned. "They all know I'm involved. They keep coming up and asking me dumb shit."

"But the shirts look nice!" she insisted. "We should put "Team Mom" on the backs or something!"

OMG. Hold on a second while my fucking nightmare comes true.

"Sure," I agreed. "But I'd like mine to say 'Please Consider Fucking Off And Not Bugging Me Mom' instead. You know, so they all know EXACTLY who they're talking to."

JTT does not play well with others. Zero Fucks Given.

The Boom:

To get through a Monday morning with minimal wailing and teeth-gnashing, I have a devised a couple of simple tricks to help you own that shit.

1. Incorporate the endearment 'muthafuckin' into every sentence.
2. Follow each sentence immediately with 'BOOM'. Your co-workers will appreciate your enthusiasm and heart your swag. Example: For breakfast, I'm having toast with muthafuckin' jelly. BOOM! See? Like a muthafuckin' boss.

I am so sick of 4th grade homework I could scream. It's too much and it's all bullshit I don't know how to DO much less explain. Tonight my 9-year old brought home some stupid-assed scholastic article about a bike ride, and his assignment was to create an outline on the topic. He pissed and moaned and bitched and griped and wrote down a bunch of words that had nothing to do with anything. In an effort to save his dumbass from himself, I erased the entire paper and said "Look. We just need to figure out four main points and then come up with a few details. Simple enough, right?" I think I was encouraging myself more than him, but whatevs. He saw where I had stripped his worksheet of all his chicken scratches and completely lost his shit. I mean, he went Mexican Kid Freaking Over Chocolate Bar batshit crazy, rolling around on the floor in a dramatic, flailing display of dismay.

"Dude. What the hell are you doing? YOU ERAZZZED THE STUFFFFF MY TEACHHERRRR TOLD ME TO WRITEEEEEEEE!!!" he sobbed.

Well, kiss my white ass. "What did she tell you to write? The main points?"

"YEZZZZZZZZ!!!!" he cried.

"Ok, when you're done acting like a douche, I'll help you fix it. In the meantime, you can borrow a fucking tampon." So he flopped around on the floor for a few more minutes, bemoaning his fate, then said (all grudging and shit)

"FINE. I'm READY for you to HELP me NOW."

Praise Jesus. I am the luckiest person in the world to get to help you with your pissy-assed attitude do some crap that I learned how to do 25 years ago and gave zero fucks about then. But I took a deep breath and said "Ok, so what was this first one?"

We figured out a few main ideas, and then without actually DOING it FOR him, I said "So what do you think is an important detail to include here?" and I calmly read the section of the article directly pertaining to that particular point.

"I DON'T REMEMBER," he moaned. "JUST TELL ME THE ANSWERRRRR."

As if. I looked him square in the eye and said "You are being a cry-ass. I. Give. Zero. Good luck with that." Then threw the pencil down and walked off.

It was a stunning exhibition of maturity and class. He was confused. "Is that the answer? Am I supposed to write that down?"

"HELL YES. WRITE THAT SHIT. WRITE IT GOOOOOD."

Which is when Mr. Tip spoke up and said to him, "Man. You messed up. It sucks to be you."

The Tiplet has since improved his attitude, begged forgiveness and is making strides to complete this pointless assignment shat from the bowels of hell.

"Ask your Dad," I suggested--firing zero fucks on all cylinders.

"Mom," he reasoned. "If Dad helps me the best I can hope for is a 'D'. He just told [my brother] that 'Betty White' knitted the first American Flag."

"Go get the paper."

The Bird and the Bank Teller

I recently found out that a local newspaper has been charging my bank account for two years for a subscription I don't have and never authorized. Now, before you say, "Don't you monitor your account?" The answer is "Hell yes. I make sure it has a fucking positive balance." If you ask, "Don't you look at the charges?" my response is "Look, a fucking squirrel!"

Anyway. I decided to call the offending newspaper and get them to stop charging my dumb ass, but they had no record of me ever having an account. So, I had to call the bank and have them fax my statements from the past 24 goddamn months. Before they could DO this, however, they had to ask me eleventy-billion questions. I'm not sure if it was my palpable frustration, or the shrillness of my voice, but the bird decided he ALSO had something to say.

Bank Person: "You realize this call is being recorded?"

Me: "Yes." Newspapers are assholes.

Bank Person: "Well, let's see what we can do to resolve this."

Bird: <RIIIIIIIINGGGGGGG> "HELLO?"

Bank Person: "Do you need to get the other line?"

Me: "No, that's okay."

Bird: "Hellllooooooo? GO TO BED. SHIT. Alright."

Bank Person: "Excuse me?"

Me: <sigh> "It's my bird. When I am on the phone, he must also be on the phone."

Bank Person: <fucking enchanted> "OMG! THAT'S AMAZING! He sounds like an actual person!"

Bird: "FUCK. SHIT. GO? GO TO BED. HELLO? COME HERE." <chirp. chirp. tweet. WHISSSSTTTTLLLLEEEEE>

Me: "Yes. He's a constant delight."

Bank Person: <laughing> "That's really a bird?"

Bird: "Good boy? Good? Ciscoooooo? Step up? SHIT. COME HERE!!!!" <smooootch> "HEY! HEY BUDDY!" <fart> <FARRRRTTTTT>

Me: "Yes. An African Grey."

Bank Person: "I must say, I can't wait for our call monitors to hear this one."

Me neither. "They will earmark my shit "Crazy Tourette's Bitch'."

And I give zero fucks.

Moustache Magnets

Rasslin is participating in an Entrepreneur Fair with the rest of the 4th graders at his school. They are studying economics, and their accompanying project is to get a loan for $20, use that to buy materials to create their product, then make enough of a profit to repay the loan, donate a portion to charity AND have spending $$ for Christmas.

My son is doing Moustache Magnets. We went and found the glass pebbles, the glue, the paper to go behind the moustaches at Walmart. (The fucking moustaches themselves which we had printed--Mr. Tip picked them up) but we were missing magnets. This meant a visit to the goddamn craft store. This place is a special kind of hell, because I always see lots of squirrels (I.E. SHIT THAT I THINK I COULD MAKE AND IT WOULD BE AWESOME AND FUN AND TURN OUT BEAUTIFULLY). Then I remember the "Scrapbooking Incident" or the "Making 80 Fucking Tied Fleece Blankets Episode" and kind of want to die.

The five of us walked in in phalanx formation, focused completely on strong, industrial strength magnets that would fit under a 1.5" pebble. I figured they would be near the beads and buttons (Look away from the fucking beads. You are NOT a jewelry designer. You do not have $427 to buy a bunch of beads to make an ugly necklace you will never wear.) But alas, the bead section was all cleared of magnets.

I had just begun admiring the iron on diamond designs (thinking that would be epic on a pair of old jeans...shut up. Don't judge me) when Velvet suggested our budding entrepreneur go ask someone for assistance.

He trotted off and found a man near the end of our aisle and told him the entire fucking story: entrepreneur fair, glass pebbles, still looking for magnets, has a football game on Saturday, do you like football, etc.

When he wandered back over to where I was rifling through the glitter letters, I mumbled, "Did you get the magnets?"

He was all, "No. I still couldn't find them. That guy I talked to didn't work here."

"You talked to him for FIVE MINUTES, Dude."

"Yeah, I know. I told him about all of the things."

"All of WHAT things? Oh look! Do we need another hot glue gun???"

"Well, one thing is how you're CRAZY."

The Squirrel Master wandered up. "LOOK MOM! GOOGLY EYES! CAN WE GET THEM???"

"Sure! Put that shit in the cart. We'll make Rudolph Candy Canes. Now we need red fuzz balls, pipe cleaners and candy canes."

"NO MOM. WE ONLY NEED MAGNETS," Velvet declared.

"Yes. We also need magnets. Where the hell do they keep the magnets??"

Just then, my eldest vagina trophy triumphantly deposited three packages of magnets in my basket. "Here Mom. I found them. Put the rest of the stuff down and walk away."

"But I...."

"FOCUS MOM!"

I am JTT and I have a problem. We only bought the magnets. But next time I'm going back without my crotchfruit to distract me.

Gnarly Bird

Tonight Mr. Tip was working, so naturally all four of my children had someplace to be simultaneously. Rah-rah had a basketball game, National Velvet had a riding lesson, Rasslin had his Magnet Sale and Stone Cold Squirrel Master had wrestling practice (which he missed because give me a fucking break already.)

After depositing the equestrian at her lesson, I took the other three to get gas because I was beyond empty. The gas station was packed. Rumor has it we're going to be getting a bit of winter weather, so even though none of these fuckwads will leave their home after the first flake falls, they must be fully gassed just in case.

I was doing a remarkable job of remaining sane despite the fact that the kid in front of me was chatting with a buddy across the lot and continued humping the pump for like 20 minutes after his shit was full. I must always admire the ZFG attitude.

Finally it was my turn.

I filled my truck in a quick and efficient manner and managed not to take off with the hose still hanging out of my gas tank. I figured that because traffic was a bitch I'd sneak through the subdivision behind the convenience store and make a nifty little short cut to drop off Rah-rah. But it was not to be.

Immediately, I found myself behind a guy who was eleventy-motherfuckin-billion years old doing a responsible 7 MPH through the city streets. I pulled over for a moment, banged my head repeatedly on the steering wheel, then pulled back behind him, patience in check. Which is when this guy STOPPED IN THE MIDDLE OF THE ROAD and just SAT THERE.

There was no oncoming traffic, there was not another car in sight. Concerned he'd died of a heart attack, I tooted my horn a bit. Immediately this old asshole whipped his gnarled hand out the window and flipped me off.

My children were stunned into silence.

Rasslin looked at me and said "Mom? Did he just give you The Bird?"

"Yes. It appears he did, Son."

"Well? What are you going to do about it? Have an arithmetic?"

"That's math. What the hell are you talking about?"

"He means 'aneurysm'," Rah-rah clarified.

I giggled. How could you not?

"WELL? What are you going to do?"

"I've considered walking up there, breaking his finger off, and shoving it up his ass. But what I'm ACTUALLY going to do is sit here, breathe deeply, and wait for him to go the fuck on to wherever he's going, and PRAY TO TINY BABY JESUS IT'S NOT THE SAME PLACE WE'RE GOING."

My children were bummed.

"Mom. You need to at least call him a douchenozzle. Cuz he is."

We were still parked in the middle of the street so I obliged. ZFG.

"MOVE THAT PIECE OF SHIT YOU OLD COOTERSNIFFER! I GOT PLACES TO BE!"

He ignored me. So I went around him. My sources say they're fairly sure he'd dumped a coffee in his lap and was dabbing at the mess he'd made of his ancient ball sack. He was indeed looking down and furiously scrubbing away at that general area. Totally worth the irritation and being late.

Put a lid on your muthafuckin' cup, Geezer.

Eyebrows

I give absolutely zero fucks about my eyebrows. The girl that does my hair has waxed them a few times and when I was on tv they tweaked that shit every now and again. I'm not much for makeup and didn't have a tweeze-a-palooza as a teen. I tend to be much more obsessed with my regular hair.

In the summer I might pause to consider my legs or pubic region. Or OMG Mr. Tip's eyebrows which have gone batshit crazy lately and I want to pluck the shit out of them. (And by 'pluck the shit out of' I mean 'accidentally shave one off'. This incident happened and has not yet been forgotten.)

I digress. Anyway, when Mr. Tip and I first got married, I had a job as a bartender. A girl that worked with me was also a part-time stripper. One night, after our shift, she invited me to go to the strip club with her and some other people from the restaurant. I called Mr. Tip and was all "We're going to the strip club after shift!" and he was all "FUCK YEAH!" so he came and picked us up and drove us to the Pussy Palace.

There was some drinking, amateur pole dancing, more drinking, kissing, vomiting...one helluva fine time. When it was time to go, the stripper/coworker friend had hooked up with a random dude from the club and wanted us to give them a ride home. I attempted to describe this desire to my husband, and he was all "Just get in the fucking truck. I'll take you home."

For some reason, he ended up bringing these people back to OUR house because they were too shitfaced to tell him where else to take them. (I have no recollection of these events. I was puking at the time.) Legend has it that he carried my drunk ass inside and put me to bed. Around fourteen hours later, I woke up and went to the kitchen for some water. Which is when I noticed the mostly naked and completely unfamiliar man candy passed out on my couch.

"WHO THE HELL ARE YOU?"

My friend (who was barely visible smashed underneath him) opened her eyes and lifted her head. I was relieved. Just as the guy was regaining consciousness she screamed, "OH MY DEAR GOD MY MOTHERFUCKING EYEBROWS!"

I was still a little buzzed and thought perhaps they were on fire or something, so I squinted and said "What the hell is wrong with your eyebrows? Why are you on my COUCH?"

Frantic, she sniffed, "Can you see them? Are they still ON THERE?" Struggling to focus, I noticed that the damn things were completely missing. There was a slight brown smear where one used to be, but the rest of them were on her new guy friend's shirt. I was beyond ecstatic.

"YOU DRAW THAT SHIT ON? I never woulda thunk it." (Which was complete horseshit. It was a constant topic of casual conversation.)

Anyway, she hadn't brought any extra brow pencil so she spent 45 minutes in the bathroom (attempting to salvage her shit with some eyeshadow I had...and she royally fucked it up) while Mr. Tip and I attempted to make awkward conversation with her boy toy.

We all went to brunch and then dropped them back at her place. Still a little queasily hungover, I said to Mr. Tip as the couple skittered inside, her hands still self-consciously covering her forehead, "I'm glad we know who we're going home with after a hard night of partying."

He stared at me. "I'm glad you have actual fucking eyebrows. And we need a new couch."

Boom.

Commando No-no

Rasslin' Tiplet had practice tonight so when we went to pick him up after school from my in-laws', Mr. Tip brought him a pile of clothes and said "Here, change."

9-year old: "I can't. Someone is in the bathroom."

Mr. Tip: "So? Change right here."

Rasslin: "I can't. Everyone will see my balls."

Mr. Tip: "How? Don't you have on underwear?"

Rasslin: "No. I didn't wear any today."

Mr. Tip: <kind of freaking the hell out> "WELL WHY NOT?!?!?"

Rasslin: "Because ummmm, ZFG?"

Well shitdamnhell. Now he dragged my ass into this mess. Mr. Tip shot me a filthy look.

Mr. Tip: "You need to wear underwear, DAMMIT. It's gross and unsanitary not to."

Me: <confused and amused> "Why do you care if he wears underwear or not?"

Mr. Tip: <sputtering> "Because he could chafe his PECKER, or get FUMUNDA cheese or ball drippings on his JEANS...DUDE. You have GOT to start wearing UNDERWEAR."

For fuck's sake. I'm all for encouraging my kid to do the right thing, but the decision to rock out with your peacock out is a goddamned personal one. I felt Mr. Tip was wayyyyy over reacting.

For example, he didn't even blink when it was discovered that one of our crotchfruit wiped their ass on a bath towel then folded it back neatly for others to use. I, on the other hand, will forevermore keep my personal towel in a hidden location to avoid a rollicking edition of "What the FUCK is that Smell? Did the Dog shit in the House? IS IT THIS TOWEL?!?!? OH MY GOD I WIPED MY FACE WITH IT!!!!"

Me: <shuddering in remembrance> "Well Judgy McJuderson. I guess we can't all be perfect like you."

Mr. Tip: "Well are YOU wearing underwear?"

Me: "Yes. As of 45 minutes ago. Before that, nope."

Rasslin: "See Dad?? I get my need for freedom from MOM."

Mr. Tip: "You have to protect your junk. Underwear is there for your PROTECTION and HEALTH."

I think what he's trying to say is, he got pantsed when he was about Rasslin's age and his scars have fucking scars. Or maybe he shit himself in class and had it not been for the toss-ability of his underwear, he would have had to call his mother. ZFG.

To end the conversation, I appealed to his sensibilities. "Dude, just satisfy your father's Nut Hut OCD and wear drawers, m'kay?"

My son considered this, then said "Ok fine, Dad. I'll start wearing underwear if you stop sleeping naked."

I think we have a Mexican standoff.

Beef Stick

7-year old: "Mom? Can I have some of your bacon?"

Me: "I don't have any bacon."

7-year old: "Yes huh. I smell it."

Me: "While that would be an awesome item to sneak and hide from you guys, I really don't have any."

10-year old: <exasperated> "He's SMELLING my BEEF STICK."

Me: "There is so much wrong with that sentence..."

10-year old: <tossing something at his brother> "Here, you can just have it."

Me: "Nicely done, Son. It never pays to be stingy with your meat."

7-year old: "Thanks! This is almost as delicious as BACON! But it's kind of making my mouth hot."

10-year old: "Mom. Stop laughing."

Me: "I'm trying. But I'm really gonna need you two to stop talking..."

Squirrely Homework

The Squirrel Master brought home his weekly class work and handed me a stack of papers to sift through.

He'd gotten several compliments on his handwriting and smiley faces throughout. He had, however received a few deducted points on a section featuring "Words That Sound Alike." (Um, can't you just say rhyming words? No? Whatever.)

1. Hen--pen (check)

2. Mouse--hause (misspelled, but yep)

3. Frog--log (woot)

4. Duck--airplane (what the hell? That doesn't sound alike at all.)

Me: "Dude? Why did you write that 'airplane' rhymes with 'duck'?"

Him: "MOM. That question was TRICKY and they wanted me to say the bad F-WORD. I am NOT writing that on a paper for at SCHOOL!"

Me: <baffled> "But there are lots of great words that rhyme with 'duck'. Truck, luck, stuck, chuck, buck, muck..."

Him: "Welp, my brain could only think of the F-WORD that rhymes with duck."

Phenomenal. I am thrilled to have influenced my seven year old's educational experience in this fashion. And certainly agree now that "airplane" is somewhat similar to "duck" after all.

They both fucking fly you know.

Onions

Mr. Tip and I have been hauling horses around since early this morning. When hauling the heavy fuckers, he likes to take his nasty, old, see-I-have-a-massive-penis-and-this-Dodge-proves-it truck. I fucking hate riding in it.

I sweated all the way through the boob area in my tank top, but gave zero fucks and went to Tractor Supply, McDonalds and to pick my kids up from school. With the insufficient a/c blowing in my face, I made my standard observation:

"This motherfucking truck stinks. What the HELL is that SMELL??"

Mr. Tip gave an obligatory sniff, glanced at the dogs and shrugged. "What's it smell like?"

"Rotted onions maybe. Like BO only worse," I informed him, indignantly.

"Check your pits," he suggested, not unkindly.

Well goddamn. Turns out I smell like the ass end of a billy goat. One that has been rolling in onions. The good news is, I found my fucking tiara and I am rocking the shit out of this bitch, smelling like ass, nary a fuck to be found.

Gloria Steinem Part 1

My 5th grader has to do a school project where she portrays a historical figure. She will prepare a monologue, dress up as her character, then line up along the hallways of her school in a living wax museum. People will peruse the halls and "push a button" to hear a short story about the person's life. She was supposed to choose five characters from a list of 70 or so that she'd like to play. She got none of them. Instead, she was assigned Gloria Steinem. My Velvet was PISSED.

Her: "NO ONE EVEN KNOWS WHO SHE IS!!"

Me: "Well, you'll have to tell them."

Her: "But she is BORING!! I don't even need a costume. Just a stupid pantsuit or something."

Me: "Bullshit. She was a Playboy bunny in the 60s. That's one of the reasons she is such an activist for women's rights. You wanna be a bunny?"

Her: "Omg. No Mom. I'd get in TROUBLE."

Me: "Why? You're portraying the character, making it interesting, I dare someone to say something."

Her: "But people will think I'm a SKANK!"

Me: "How so? You're Gloria in the 60s. We can do it tastefully. And PLENTY of people will listen to your monologue."

Her: <considering> "Well, your ideas hardly ever suck. Let's do it!!"

Which is why I just bought fishnet stockings and muthafuckin' bunny ears for my 11-year old's school project. I kick ass at this parenting thing.

Gloria Steinem Part 2

Velvet is depicting Gloria Steinem for her 5th Grade school project. I convinced her to dress as a playboy bunny ala GS in the 60s. She was hesitant. She didn't want to look like a slut, and she has quite a figure for her age. So I bought her a robe with the bunny logo on the back, and she will wear ears, heels and fishnets (as well as shorts and a tank under the robe). The robe arrived yesterday.

Rah-rah was freaking ecstatic. She ripped her clothes off, donned the pink, rabbity confection (and my 5" stripper heels) and began prancing around the living room. Because the ears had not yet arrived she substituted her mouse ears but everyone got the idea.

Mr. Tip: "Holy shit." <pressing his lips together in a pissy line> "What the fuck have you DONE?"

Me: <trying not to pee from all the laughing> "I am supporting my daughter's school project."

Him: "THAT'S THE WRONG DAUGHTER!! God save us. She has your legs."

It was Velvet's turn to don the costume. She is much more modest (and boobiliscious) than her sister. So she put it on and stood there, somewhat self-conscious, looking around 25 or so. Mr. Tip turned to me, with a mixture of disgust and horror. "We are so fucked." Yup. Super-fucking fucked. Suddenly, I think he identified a bit more with my father-- who also had to deal with lots of legs, boobs and ZFG when my sister and I were younger.

Just then, Rasslin' emerged from the shower, hair a spiky mess, wearing my old silk pajama cover. "This thing is smooth on my butt!!" he declared, stroking his ass.

I think they get this from me.

All hail.

It's All Fun and Games

Once upon a time, my eldest son, brushing up on his prankster skills, shoved his way into a tight closet area where I was trying to get shit organized. "What the hell are you doing?" I asked, genuinely confused. None of his personal items were in jeopardy due to my organizational burst of energy, and it is very unlike any of my spawn to chance getting roped into an unpleasant task.

"Ah, I just missed you, Mom," he said sweetly. In a rare, blissful see-kids-can-actually-ENHANCE-your-life moment, my suspicions melted away and I said "Awww. I missed you too, Dude!" We were all fucking Beaver Cleaver and shit for a few seconds, before I went back to finding matches for all of the goddamn pairs of shoes I never wear.

We continued in silence for a few minutes. "Oh, what's that?" my loin-spawn inquired, reaching under some jeans I'd piled in the corner. "What's it look like?" I answered distractedly, wondering if perhaps a mouse had made a nest using part of my wool boot socks. Which is when my son screamed like a bitch. As I looked to see how to protect this defenseless man-child who once lived inside of me, a rat-esque form launched itself straight at my face. I had a full-blown panic attack, tore down half of my hung clothing and nearly broke my femur attempting to escape the flying rodent.

Still not sure if it was actually ON ME, I was seizing and twisting and making a high pitched "eeeeeeaaaeeee" sound. Which was about the time I realized Rasslin's mirth. He was laughing so goddamn hard no sound was coming out, and he was pointing at the source of my angst. It was one of Eleanor Rigby's fucking bastard catnip mice. The little shit has jokes. Funny, funny jokes. Once my heart rate stabilized and I was mostly certain I wasn't going to need the paddles after all, I smiled at my crotch monkey and said this: "Payback is a bitch, my friend."

"BUT I GOT YOU MOM, I GOT YOUUUUUU!!!" So you did, you little asswipe. But mark my words. Payback. Is. A. Bitch. Then I let it go. (And by "let it go" I mean I refused to go in the master closet ever again, threw out all of the cat's toys resembling vermin and have fallen asleep many times plotting revenge.)

Tonight I was presented with a golden gem of an opportunity.

Payback's a Bitch

My tired kid fell asleep on the couch shortly after Mr. Tip came home from work. Usually I will make him go to his bed (because Cisco does not appreciate sharing his bedroom with anyone and he makes this fact known at the ass-slit of dawn when I am trying to sleep) and also because I like to know where everyone is in the event of an emergency.

I didn't even know Rasslin' was on the sofa until I'd ventured into the kitchen to find a snack (whoever bought the pecan halves is a muthafuckin' genius). Munching on a handful of nuts, I gently shook Rasslin'. "Hey. Did you go pee before you went to sleep?" He ignored me. "I don't want you to piss on the couch, Dude. Get up and go to the bathroom."

Still no response. "Do you want me to carry you to your bed?" Nothing.

"Dammit." <pause for effect> "Ok then. Just stay there." <gently laying an uneaten pecan half on his bare shoulder>

"WHOA. That's a BIG-ASSED BUG!" This declaration prompted a minuscule shrug which dislodged the setting pecan and it fell down his shoulder alongside his back.

My son immediately snapped to complete consciousness, vaulted himself off the couch in a tizzy and allowed the horror to register on his face as the brown, large-bug-sized nut slid to the ground. He was slapping at his back, bucking like a crazed mule and trying to see the offending insect when he noticed me wiping my eyes and struggling to breathe. Peering at the fallen object Rasslin mumbled, "Is that a dead beetle or one of those nuts?"

"That's payback," I giggled.

"For the mouse?" he wondered, still struggling to find his bearings.

"Yes. And for ignoring me."

"Welp," he sighed. "I don't have to pee anymore now."

"Ewww," I groaned. "You pissed yourself?"

"Just a little," he assured me, yawning. "Yours was better than my mouse one. My next one will have to be the most epic prank of all time."

Oh God. I thought we were EVEN. What the hell have I done?? I'm too old for this bullshit. And you know what they say about payback.

Let Er Happen

It's time to share with you a legend from way back--before I was born. This is one of those tales that has been told and retold at gatherings and always elicits fits of giggles and is the basis for a popular family motto or two.

My grandfather was Type A diabetic. He was relatively young when he was diagnosed, and was insulin dependent for his entire adult life. He gave precisely zero fucks. He'd test his sugar and administer the appropriate dose when needed, then go on about his business. His wife, on the other hand, was a Sugar Nazi.

My great-grandparents lived in a small town where my mother was raised, so before my parents started collecting loinspawn, they would often make the weekend trek with her parents to visit their cute little farm. There was a local bakery. This bakery had the best muthafuckin' donuts in the history of the world. So on Saturday mornings, my dad and Peepaw would drive and collect these deep fried mouth orgasms and bring them back to share. They always purchased two dozen. One for the pair of them (to be eaten undetected by the Sugar Nazi) and one for everyone else.

They had a secret place they would hang out...a quaint boat dock on the river where they could watch the people swim, the boats go out and the kids dick around in the surf. One lazy Saturday morning, they were chillin' on the dock eating fistfuls of sweet glory, when my dad suggested they pack it in. "Gimme one more," Peeps held out his hand. My dad handed it to him and settled back in slightly antsy for a few more minutes away from the womenfolk. As they were sitting there, it happened. A pair of young men arrived in a convertible Cadillac--fresh off the showroom floor. They were towing a brand-spanking new speedboat, fresh from the marina. These boys had struck gold and they were ballin'. Hard.

There was a pair of scantily clad women sitting up on the trunk like a couple of contenders for "Miss Gutter Slut USA". "Are you ready now?" my dad asked, mindful of the fact he was pushing the hell out of that imposed newlywed time limit and was not excited about pissing my mother off. "Hold on a minute," Peepaw suggested wisely. "Shit's about to get good." My father sighed, glanced at his watch and resigned himself to a longer wait.

It didn't take long for the two buffoons to capture his interest. One got out of the car so as to guide the driver as he attempted to maneuver the boat into the water. "BACKER IN DERE, MATEY!!" shouted the partner on the shore, decked out in his new boat shoes and captain's hat. "HOLD ON CAPTAIN! Get DA WOMEN in DA VESSEL first!" At this, the bitches slid off the side of the car, tottered carefully to the trailer hitch and allowed themselves to be hoisted into the watercraft, giggling and trying desperately to avoid any molecule of water touching their lithe forms.

"What the hell?" Dad questioned. "Epic shit," my grandfather replied, knowledgeably. Somehow they got the boat in the water and Matey managed to park the pimpmobile. He then trotted to the water's edge, sat on his ass and proceeded to carefully don a pair of water skis. "LACE EM UP TIGHT!" shouted The Captian. "YESSIR!" replied Matey. Leaning back in his chair, now in shock and awe, my dad said, "Is he going in DRY?" "SHHHHHHHH," Peeps admonished. "I can't hear with you beating your damn gums." So Matey put on his water skis and stood on the edge of the river. The Captain tossed him a ski rope that was still in the package, and fixed his end to the speedboat. The women tittered and pranced to their respective places and settled in for the Matey's debut as Waterski Magee.

The crowd that had gathered all agreed that this was likely their first time ever attempting this death-defying feat. "ARE YA READY, MATEY?" shouted the Captain, revving his craft, moistening the crotches of bikini babes everywhere. "I'M A READY!" answered Matey, adjusting his gloves and holding tight to the end of the rope. "LET 'ER HAPPEN, CAPT'N!!" At this, the Captain threw the hammer down, causing the boat to stand straight up in the air. The women shrieked and grabbed for purchase to avoid being tossed overboard. And the Matey stood, grinning like an asshole, as his rope quickly uncoiled and eventually ran out of slack. "GodDAYUM," murmured my dad as the inertia finally caught up to the fuckwad standing on the shore holding his rope--his arms were jerked clean out of their sockets as he skipped along the wake like a glorious screaming stone.

"CAPPPPTTTTAAAAAAIIIIIINNNNNNNNN!!!" he screeched, finally letting go, and damn near drowning before a passing fisherman dragged his dumbass out of the depths.

This is where the legend gets fuzzy. In some versions a twank is thrown from the boat in the initial takeoff. In others, the Captain rides into the sunset, purveyor of all the snatch minus a first mate. The truth is no one gives a fuck because at this point we're all laughing too hard at poor Matey's misfortune. I can tell you this: if ever the words, "LET ER HAPPEN, CAPT'N" are uttered around here, shit just got really real. Better grab life vest.

The Peacock Discussion

Mr. Tip and I finally had The Peacock Discussion.

Him: <resigned and incredulous> "Are you REALLY fucking getting peacocks? That ranks among the DUMBEST shit you've ever done. Ever."

Me: "Bullshit. You always think my ideas are dumb. You raised hell when I bought Meg, too, and look what an integral part of our lives she has become!"

Him: "Yes, but these are FUCKING PEACOCKS. You do not know how to take care of them, and they're going to get KILLED or grow up and you'll HATE them. And I will be stuck tending the fucking peacocks."

Me: "You can borrow my sucking rod. In case they attack you. My peacocks will be badass."

Him: <pleading> "Please don't get peacocks. Get another dog. Keep Rosa Barks. Save another horse. Have a donkey. Find another cat. I could give a shit. But peacocks will be nothing but headache and heartache."

Me: "You always try to steal my joy. But I am The Queen of Peacocks. The Khaleesi could not be The Mother of Dragons without a motherfucking dragon. Consider my image. JTT Nation. The universe's alignment. MY WANTS AND NEEDS."

Him: "I would rather you get anything other than a bunch of peacocks."

Me: "What about a baby? Not like you 'planting the crotchfruit' and me growing that shit, but like if one turned up in a trashcan somewhere or on the front step. Could we adopt it? I always wanted to adopt a baby."

Him: "OR A BABY GODDAMMIT. NO BABIES."

Me: "You are yelling at me. For no reason. Another parrot?"

Him: "You're crazy."

Me: "Insanity is a virtue. As are peacocks. Who historically belong to royalty and floof their tails and amuse them."

Body Modification

Rah-rah: "Mom? Would you be mad if I got my belly button pierced?"

Me: "Nah. I don't much care about piercings. As long as the place that does it is clean. Dad would be pissy though. He doesn't like them."

Rasslin': "He doesn't like belly buttons? You totally have your nose pierced. Dad likes THAT, doesn't he? "

Me: "I don't know. I never asked him."

Rah-rah: "Well, I don't want someone stabbing a needle through part of my stomach."

Me: "Then a piercing is probably not for you."

Velvet: "I don't like those ones where they stretch them out so there is a big hole in your earlobe, like big enough to put your finger through. I think that must really hurt."

Me: "Hmmm. I don't think I'd ever personally do one of those, but they don't really hurt, I don't think. You just get bigger plugs and stretch them slowly over time. If I DID do one, though, I'd get a little lizard to ride around in the gauge. I'd name him Prince Edmund."

Rasslin': <considering> "Why would you name him that? I like the name 'Fred' for an ear lizard. I think the ultimate piercing would be if someone put a doorknob in their cheek."

Me: "Or a bike peg in their thigh" <referencing Rasslin's bike stunt-gone-wrong that landed him in the ER and with an assload of stitches.>

Rasslin': "Yeah. That one was AWESOME. At least chicks dig scars."

Me: "I guess. But you don't need to be showing chicks that high up your thigh, Playa."

Rasslin': "Well how else are they SUPPOSED TO SEE IT?"

Me: "They have to take your word for it."

Velvet: <switching back to the body mod> "I bet lip piercings hurt the worst."

Me: "Probably no more than a cold sore or something. I think getting your schnitzel pierced would be painful."

Rasslin': "PEOPLE PIERCE THEIR DANGLES??? Why would someone DO that? HOW DO THEY EVER TAKE A WHIZ AFTER THAT?"

Littlest: <joining in the convo quite late in the game and missing the point> "You need to ask Dad how boys pee. Mom doesn't know. Mom pees like a girl."

Rah-rah: "OMG, DAD HAS AN EARRING IN HIS PACKAGE?"

Me: <failing to defend Mr. Tip's jewley-free joystick> "Well, I don't think if it's in your man meat, it's technically an EARRING."

Velvet: "I don't want to know WHAT it's called. I want to know why in the world you would EVER LET HIM do something like that."

Me: "Wellllllll, I didn't ask his permission to get my NOSE pierced."

Rah-rah: "I can't believe we're talking about this."

I can't believe my crotchfruit are convinced Mr. Tip has a bar in his trouser mouse.

Diagnosing the Master of Squirrels

My youngest child has Attention Deficit Disorder. He sees all of the squirrels and forgets all of the tasks and wandered around in La-la Land for the entire year of Kindergarten and most of first grade. After the initial grading period, Mr. Tip and I came in for a teacher conference and it was The Talk I'd been dreading since I enrolled my child in Kindergarten.

They were going to tell me he was fucked up. He couldn't do the work. He was falling behind. They were going to try to convince me to medicate him...muddle his brain, change him to fit society's definition of normal. I cried a lot. I held Mr. Tip's hand tightly and shook and contemplated vomiting on the tiny desk I was perched on. For his part, my husband was like "Oh yeah, well, what were we talking about again?" because he ALSO has ADD and because well, SQUIRRELS.

We made Littlest an appointment with a pediatrician and he quickly boasted an official ADD diagnosis, so we had to decide how to proceed. We removed red dye from his diet, as well as most sugars and some other blah blah bullshit that supposedly exacerbates symptoms. I blamed myself, I blamed my husband, I blamed my older children for being normal and leaving my sweet baby behind. He still struggled.

Homework that should have taken him ten minutes to complete took fucking HOURS. It was like his brain was just TOO DAMN BUSY to get the shit done so he could go play, tweak, chase squirrels. I dreaded him coming home at all because I was bracing for a fight. And I typically got my wish.

Finally we agreed to try him on a low dose of something and I almost shit my pants over the difference I noticed immediately in my son. Not only was he focused, but he was SMART. He wanted to learn about ALL of the things. He could give me answers and skip over pages of explanations and move on to things that interested him like Earthquakes and Storms and Treefrogs and Squirrels. Math and

Science came easy to him. Reading did not (which tears at my very soul because that's something that I can help him with) but each night he would muddle through a book.

When you are blessed with a child that experiences the world differently than you do, you're forced to take a good, hard look at yourself. You wonder how you can help them to realize what really matters and you never expect them to actually teach YOU what you've been missing your entire life. Tonight my littlest boy crawled up in the bed with me and said "Mom. I'm going to read you a story, okay?" It was not okay.

It was past his bedtime and when HE wants to read then I end up correcting his words and I worry he'll never get it and I worry he won't care and I end up giving all the fucks anyway and crying because he can't do it right. I had other shit to do. I did NOT have time to feel like a parental failure while my baby read me a book.

"Dude, I don't much feel like reading tonight. Can we save it for tomorrow?"

He sighed. "What if you don't have to read and I read it TO YOU?"

Yeah, I was afraid of that. "Sure. Read it, Bud."

So he opens the book and starts reading about a little boy who goes to his Grandmother's house and doesn't have any of his overnight things and Granny has to make him a bed and a pillow and a fucking teddy bear...it's one of my favorites.

He didn't miss a word. I have NEVER loved that story as much as I loved it tonight, with my son reading it, placing emphasis where it belonged, assigning voices and mannerisms to the characters, delighting when I genuinely giggled at his performance. About halfway through the story, I started crying like a fucking asshole.

"MOMMY, WHAT'S WRONG??? This is a HAPPY story! Why are you sad?"

"I'm NOT sad," I wailed, wiping my nose on his sleeve. "I'm just HAPPY that you are the BEST reader EVER."

"Well," he shrugged. "It's probably because I got the best mom to teach me how to read it right!"

Holding my boy close to me, looking at this book together, I realized I was experiencing a tiny miracle. I always knew he WOULD eventually read, but I figured he would HATE it. And yet, there we were enjoying this story he selected because he knew I liked it.

He read EVERY WORD. I realize I am blessed. I can't count the blessings they are so plentiful. But tonight I'm glad I took the time. To listen. To let my baby show me what he's been working on.

He's leaving me...gaining his independence, becoming his own person, growing up. But he still wants to share his triumphs. When the story was over, I said, "Man, they never DID get to go to bed at all the WHOLE NIGHT! I bet they're ready for breakfast, don't you?"

He agreed that perhaps a breakfast would be a suitable next chapter in the story. "Want me to make you some butter biscuits with cinnamon? We can eat them in my bed and watch TV and pretend it's Breakfast Time!!"

"No, we are NOT ALLOWED to eat cinnamon in your bed because is messes up the blankets with CRUMBS!"

"Yeah, but the girls are coming tomorrow to clean up for us. Let's give them something good to clean. You get the butter, I'll make the cinnamon."

And that's why we're waiting for those bitches to finish baking, so we can slather them with all of the messy deliciousness, then sit under the covers and eat them while we watch something awesome like "Cops" or "Naked and Afraid." I will never ever forget. Please tell your crotchfruit how much they mean to you...how they enhance your life...and how fucking bored you'd be without them in it.

Peace, Love and AFG <3

JTT Hotel Stay

One of the best parts about a JTT hotel stay is interacting with (and by "interacting with" I clearly mean fucking with) the staff. It began this morning when the Hispanic HB Brigade busted up in my digs at 8:12am. "OH MEEES WE SO SORRRRY COME BACK, COME BACK!!!" And I'm all "No need. Just tidy around my sleeping ass. And can you make the bed with me in it?" They no habla-ed and beat a hasty retreat, but did leave me loads of extra towels and shampoos. Then when I returned from my day's outing, my room key didn't work and neither did the ice machine. I was more distraught about the ice maker. So I trotted up to the front desk.

Me: "My key isn't working."

ZFG counter guy: "What's your room number?"

Me: "I think it's 114. But it might be 118. It's right across from the ice machine which is also not working."

Him: <taking my key and doing some magic reactivation> "That's 114."

Me: "Don't you want to see my ID?"

Him: "Naw, I remember you."

Me: "Well, don't remember some perv who also has a broken key for 114."

Him: <grinning> "Ok. There is another ice machine on the third floor."

Me: "Um, bullshiz. If I wanted to exercise, I'd go to the fitness room with my card that is now working. As it IS, I just want to walk my happy ass across the hall and fill my drinkie-drink with ice."

Him: "We have an elevator..."

Me: "OH HELL NO. YOU HAVE TOO MUCH BREAKING SHIT FOR ME TO JUMP ON A HELLEVATOR FOR SOME DAMN ICE."

HIM: <finally laughing...fucking tough crowd today> "Come on, let's go look at it."

Me: "Chop-chop. The vodka's getting hawt."

So we go to the ice machine and he reaches up inside of it and a bunch of ice falls out and it's fixed like a miracle.

Me: "YOU FIXED IT!" <clapping wildly>

Him: <shrugging> "Yeah, sometimes you gotta reach up there and feel around and knock it loose. Then it works again."

Me: <thoughtfully> "So kind of like a woman, huh?"

Him: <shocked then laughing> "You are officially my favorite guest of all time."

Me: "It took you an agonizingly long time to figure that shit out, huh?"

Him: "My bad. Do you need anything else?"

Me: "I could go for a muffin. A blueberry one. With butter."

Him: <shaking his head> "Breakfast is over at 10. It's after 5."

Me: "It's 10:00 somewhere..."

And Boom. Muffin time, bitches.

Muthafuckin Waffle Maker

I have three words for you: Muthafuckin Waffle Maker. It is the possession of this appliance that awards any hotel that offers a continental breakfast an additional four stars in my book. I love that shit. This morning I got up and went to grope and violate my ice machine (which is still somewhat temperamental but really only needs an occasional manual molestation to produce loads of cubes). I heard a major dick-swinging grand time being had in the lobby, so despite the fact that I bra less, barefooted, and looked like I'd just crawled from under a rock after a three day bender, I sauntered up in the midst of that bitch.

There were about twenty dudes decked out in their formal business wear, sipping their gourmet French press latte shit, blah-blahing about important business happenings and eating these dainty little bran muffins (presumably to take a perfectly timed conference dump later this morning.) But then I saw the waffle maker. The Heavens smiled. The angels sang. And my starvation level went from a "meh, I could stand a bite to eat" to "MUST MASTICATE EVERY CARB IN THE BUILDING. WHERE IS THE GODDAMN SYRUP?? DO I FILL THIS MEASURING CUP TO THE BRIM?!?! STAND ASIDE SMALL RANDOM SNOT-NOSED CHILD WHO MAY ALSO ENJOY A WAFFLE BUT IT IS NOT YOUR FUCKING TURN YET. WATCH AND LEARN WHILE I SHOW YOU ALL OF MY SKILLZ."

Then I didn't put enough raw waffle in. Then I was too stupid to flip it over. Then I almost burned my goddamn hand off trying to peek and check the readiness. I was so blond, ding batted and ratchet-looking that three executively suited and bespectacled dudes sat aside their Starbucks, newspapers and cell phones to collectively create the most de-fuckin-lish waffle in the History of Waffles. One even removed his blazer --and rolled up his sleeves. Pour that batter, Baby. Fry it up right.

Ballsacktomy

We took the kids out to eat. It was crowded (Sunday night, duh) and we were seated at a large round table so it wasn't easy to hear everyone unless you were directly next to them. I was discussing something completely random with Rasslin' (tuning out the Tiplet chatter around me) when I heard Mr. Tip declare "There is NOTHING WRONG with MAKING LOVE to the person you're MARRIED TO."

Except of course for calling it "making love" and not "laying some pipe" or "fucking like rabbits." I maintain that frank and open talks are most effective when proper terminology is used.

"Oh GAWD. What are you talking about?" I gasped, throwing down my chopsticks trying not to choke on an egg roll. This was not the time to discuss our "lovemaking" or "Humpfests" (seriously, Honey...) with our crotchfruit. Mr. Tip took a moment to compose himself. He is finally getting used to his trio of lovely ladies lamenting about riding the cotton pony, bra sizing and raging synchronized hormones, but sex discussions leave him in dire need of a tequila shot or ten.

"Rah-rah said the only reason I had a vasectomy was so I could do dirty things with you and not get you pregnant," he spat.

Indignant. Insulted. When he gives me the business it is a thing of BEAUTY and GRACE goddammit. I put my hand on my chest. "You mean we've been DOING ALL THOSE NASTY THINGS and I don't even have A CHANCE of getting knocked up? WHY WOULD YOU KEEP THIS FROM ME?? What if I want another BABY?"

My daughters gaped open-mouthed, both delighted by the drama and disgusted by the veiled admission of "doing dirty things." But I feel it is important to be supportive of my sweetie as he trudges through these uncomfortable pubescent questions posed by his mini-JTTs. "Stoppit," he hissed.

All of this came up because he told the girls (a long assed time ago) that we wouldn't have more kids because he'd been 'fixed'. They assumed that (as in the animal kingdom) this meant he had his testicles removed. When they shared this assumption on some random Mr. Tip-less car ride one lazy afternoon a million years ago, I was delighted (yet another glorious mothering motto--never correct shit that makes you laugh) and deliberately neglected to set them straight. So somehow, this all came out in the middle of muthafuckin P.F. Chang's right when the server was bringing my muthafuckin pepper steak. I suggested we table the inquisition for a more private time (like at his parents' house during a formal gathering of some sort) and it was dropped.

With grumbles and sighs of repulsion from my ladyspawn, but the subject changed. Mr. Tip's parting suggestion was to look up "vasectomy" on google to quell all of the curiosities and answer all of the medical queries either might have regarding his procedure. Velvet rolled her eyes. "It's not on google, Dad. We HAVE looked. 'Ballsacktomy' has like three results and none of them have ANYTHING to do with birth control."

Excuse me...I'm going to need a pair of tequila shots for him and a bottle of vodka--straight up, for me. Anyway, I'm pretty sure we learned three things from this enlightening family dysfunction.

1. I am going to Hell.

2. Mr. Tip is not prepared for three of me.

3. Raising teenagers is way fucking harder than raising toddlers. They eat dirt, fall off furniture, stick their fingers in a light socket, meltdown in the middle of Target over a sucker, but they do not inquire about the details of their father's ballsacktomy.

Homemade Pasties

Last night, it was hot as leather-clad Congo balls. I swore (when it snowed in March) that I would not complain about the heat this summer and I WON'T, but I'll bitch about the humidity all day. So I put on my black dress. This lovely enigma is my favorite--one of those softies that defy the need for undergarments of any kind. It's all FLOWY and lightweight and glorious. I figure people who are blatantly gaping at me are staring at my tan.

Velvet had a schooling show. It's kind of a 'pretend' show. The classes are set up like they would be in a 'real' show, except the instructors yell pointers while riders do their thing in the ring. Parents are invited and typically clap politely after each student completes their turn. Da Queen and her extended entourage (conversely) took the encouragement to a whole new level.

We would hoot and holler wildly after each performance and attempted to enhance their chances of a WIN (my crotchfruit included) with creative tips to REALLY impress the judges. A well timed backflip off their pony, for example or a fabulous galloping dismount with a somersault for extra flair. (This must be completed with a "Ta-da!!" though or points deducted cuz you just look like a fucking bowling ball coming off your Equine Asshat.)

I was slightly self conscious about my nipples showing (even though the dress is black and it hides most things). You know, a side view could spook a horse or worse distract one of the dads attempting to watch his princess's equitation evolution--not stare at the crazy bitch who kept suggesting her daughter attempt an Ariel Twist whilst her steed was at the apex of his flight over the poles. (What is the point of a SCHOOLING show if one CANNOT OFFER POINTERS?) Completely sans bra was not an option. A strapless bra was also not an option because I don't have a black one, and because to wear a bra would be to shit on the amazing softness that is this dress. Luckily, I have a few tricks.

Me: "Girls!! Who has a pantyliner?"

Squirrel Master: "What's a 'panty flamer'?"

Me: "Your dad."

Mr. Tip: <oblivious, embracing all of his inner squirrels on some wildly entertaining game on his phone>

Rah-rah: "Why do you need a pantyliner?"

Me: "Because I do."

Rah-rah: "I don't have any."

Velvet: "There are some in your bathroom. I saw them."

So a pantyliner was procured and everyone gathered around to watch the magic unfold. I simply cut circles out of either end and had instant pasties that tamed the boobie boners for good.

Velvet quickly started rocking out the ribbons--four to be exact, so my tips were well covered and my rack was complimented many times as Best in Show. Fun for all.

Once we returned home and it was time to remove my clever little secret, I did the whole Bandaid rip removal and almost tore my fucking nipple off. "OH HOLY SHIT," I wailed, eyes watering, fucks flying everywhere. I peered cautiously at my poor, abused nip and ascertained it had suffered no permanent damage. It was red and slightly gluey, but having fed Tiplets, I can assure you, that bitch has actually already been through Hell.

I checked the pantyliner box, just to see if Gorilla Glue was a listed ingredient. Nope, though the box DID boast "Extra sticky". To keep those motherfuckers staying put wherevah they ended up. My second nipple fared no better than the first but at least I knew to brace for it. When I wear the damn dress again, it will be completely bare under there. Because ZFG. (Sometimes I forget my own damn motto. But I never stop loving it.)

All hail The Queen but be cautious of her traumatized tips.

Pussy Lovers

Velvet has been working for her trainer this summer in exchange for lessons. She hacks several horses a day, cleans tack and stalls, grooms ponies and at the tender age of 11 is learning that shit worth having is worth working for. She has to be there around the ass-crack of dawn. This morning was no exception. Except that I didn't want to drive anywhere or do anything but SLEEP. But she made me coffee. And brought me pants. And hurried me along. "MOM. I am going to be LATE." <sigh> And I am going to remind you of this when I am old and need a diaper change.

A few minutes later she returned. "Mom. I hear kittens." ZFG for fucking kittens. It's the cats from up the road again. Don't feed them and I'll have one of the other kids take them home when I get back from taking you. "No. THOSE kittens are on the front porch. I hear THESE under the back deck." I don't care. Where are we on that coffee?

As I dragged my pants on and debated a bra, she burst through my door sobbing. "MOM THERE ARE BABIES IN THE BACKYARD AND THE DOGS ARE KILLING THEM PLEASE PLEASE HELP ME!!" Goddammit all to fucking hell and back. No. No. Nonononono. I reject this information. But I hauled ass to the backyard. Indeed the dogs had been dogs. A few tiny bodies lay littered about the yard and my heart just shattered (like it does. All of the fucks.) When there is a crisis I try to get shit organized--dogs over there (you stupid bastard asshole baby-killing fuckwads) and locate the survivors who are wailing their feline whiskers off...well. FUCK.

With Velvet behind me heaving huge sobs I told her to look for the others and I gathered the tiny mauled bodies. One was not yet dead (which is even fucking worse because now I have to wait for it to die and GODDAMMIT STUPID DOGS) but she was still so I laid her with the others on the ledge of the dog house. I found one survivor raising hell next to the steps. The other, while vocal in his displeasure, was not nearly so willing to expose himself, so I got to army crawl under the mud pit beneath the deck filled with shit and standing water and one tiny black mewling kitten.

Covered in muck, I emerged with the kitten, and by this point Velvet had roused her sister who was pointing out the still moving form with the fallen. Great. Let's bring it inside to die. It's little body was clearly broken, I could feel the distention when I picked it up. I called Mr. Tip, had a full blown melt-down panic attack and demanded he call Velvet's trainer and explain her absence. "OH NO. I still have to go, Mom!" "I'll stay," Rah-rah said simply. "The boys are asleep. I'll stay with the kittens. Hurry back." This was not how I wanted my girl to experience death...alone. I told her to put the injured baby in the basket with a warm towel and to focus on the extremely dehydrated other two.

Then I called my regular small animal vet. I freaking love the people that care for my animals there. But the receptionist is a fucking CUNT. For the second time in as many months, she made a fatal error. The receptionist saw no reason for my frantic distress. Her suggestion to put them in with their mother (WHAT MOTHER? AND WHERE? THE GODDAMN DOGS WERE EATING THEM YOU ASSMAGGOTTED SNATCH!! ARE WE HAVING SOME FAILURE TO COMMUNICATE???) was met with a calm and very un-JTT "No you don't understand. I'd like a vet to take a look at them." "Oh. <huge sigh> Let me put you on hold." Amazingly, I waited. I assumed she was speaking with a vet or someone with at least a fuck to spare. Finally she returned. "Well it will cost $49.50 for the office visit before they are even treated. That will not cover any care they may need. We do not offer discounts for strays."

I may have lost my shit. I may have said "You money-grubbing whore, I did not ask you how much it would cost. I did not ask you to be my fucking accountant. I asked you to get me in to see the goddamn vet." "Oh, I'M SORRY, but you said..." I know what I said. Hear this, "Fuck you, Bitch." End scene.

I called another clinic (whom I do not have an account with) and the suggestion was made to try some soft food and water and see if they eat. Exasperated, I called one more small animal vet. I explained the situation.

"Where is the mother?" They asked.

"I don't know," I answered.

"Are they worth looking at?"

"Absolutely."

"We are waiting for you. Get here when you can."

I tore in to the parking lot (slowed momentarily by a woman going FUCKING THREE MPH before she FINALLY PARKED and unfastened the seatbelt HOLDING HER CAT CARRIER) goddammit... move. The vet was waiting. Despite some dehydration, the two surviving kitties were going to be okay. Still breathing, the broken clinger mewed pitifully. Which is when I started crying. Fell apart a little. "It's okay," the vet soothed me. "You can leave them here. The techs will feed them." I shook my head. "They're mine," I whispered. "They were trusted to me. And I failed them." The tech hugged me. "YOU DID GOOD!" She smiled. LOOKIT these pretty babies!

The vet continued examining the dying kitten. "Please don't make it suffer." "Yeah, let's give it a shot." Fuck. Here it comes. I hate euthanasia. "It should help with the pain. I think she got rolled around and broke a couple of ribs, but her lungs are clear and a grievous internal injury would have killed her by now."

What? This baby has a chance? ALL FUCKING IN, BABY!! Let me show you how many fucks I can give at ONCE. We left with a bottle of milk replacer and instructions to feed them every few hours or when they are hungry. They are estimated to be only a couple of weeks old, but were quite dehydrated. I rejected the offer to discount the services. I usually do. They were mine the second I heard them cry.

As we were leaving, I noticed the woman who had been all the hell up in my way as we were trying to get in the building. She had a tissue box and huge tear-filled eyes. She was bringing her pussy-pal of 16 years in to say goodbye. And I was rushing and cursing and snarling caught up in my own crisis. Normally this realization would not affect me because ZFG. But this morning, the stars aligned.

Despite much resistance and eye-rolling, I've come to realize and accept that they are 'mine' for a reason. Probably so I may go completely broke one wounded un-human vaginaspawn at a time, but a reason nonetheless. I left the tech with my personal information should the grieving woman need it 'for any reason' in the near future, the woman herself with a hug and a basketful of meowing fucks. I am such a goddamned sucker. And still not a cat person at all. But definitely a pussy lover ;)

Holiday World

I am in charge of finding a place to stay overnight. This has been my job since the dawn of time because I give all of the fucks and Mr. Tip gives zero. Actually, he got to pick one time and went totally budget and we ended up sleeping huddled on a damp MATTRESS. And by "we" I mean me, Rah-rah (who was two) my sister (who was a teenager) and Velvet (who was still in an infant seat that I wouldn't take her out of because MRSA and shit).

Mr. Tip sat by the door with a gun all night. There was no bathing because of a suspicious red stain in the tub...oh gawd. My fucking scars have scars. So I pick the place now. He rolls his eyes and if necessary, I remind him of the night we spent in the fuckin' hood. I called a few potential lodges (with in house day spas because duh) and they were booked, so I settled on a hotel that offered suites...two beds with a pull out couch.

We have stayed with this particular chain many times and while they lack a masseuse, they DO have a belgian waffle maker (which is almost as awesome).

This is how the conversation went:

Me: "Do you have any suites available Tuesday night?"

Poor Dude Stuck Working the Phone: "Yes ma'am! I'm showing a king suite with a sleeper and two queens with a sleeper sofa."

Me: "Well, I'm the Queen of Errythang, so I guess I'll take the queens."

Him: "Okay. Would you like the newly renovated room?"

Me: "Duh. Also, can you please make sure our room has a door that separates the sleeping area from the living room?"

Him: <crestfallen> "Oh, I'm sorry. Those rooms are being renovated currently."

Me: "Ok. I'll take one of those."

Him: <confused> "But they aren't available. Only our very spacious one room suites are open."

Me: "Well where am I supposed to perform my wifely duties? I need to close the door for true."

Him: <silence>

Me: "Hello?"

Him: <flustered or laughing> "So can I put you down for the one room suite?"

Me: "Dude, I'm traveling with four kids. How am I supposed to hump my husband without a door to separate us from our crotchfruit?"

Him: <considering> "Well, there is a door to the bathroom. I think if you are quiet that might work for you."

Me: <OMG SO MUCH WIN!!> "I guess."

Him: <typing> "So you're a newlywed?"

Me: "Yep. We've only been married fifteen years."

Him: "YEARS??"

Me: "Yeah, I guess that's fairly new."

Him: "I've only been married for seven months. I hope my wife and I have the same passion in fifteen years..."

Me: "Well, it mostly depends on the wife. Alrighty then. I'm pretty much done screwing with you...have you got all my shit you need?"

Him: "Yes I will send your confirmation."

Me: "Thank you. You've been very helpful."

Him: "And you have been the best caller I've ever had."

Me: "Yeah. I get that a lot. It's good to be Queen."

Boom.

Customer Service

It was late when we arrived at our hotel Tuesday night. Because good things happen to those who love the Lord, the same schmo I'd booked the room with the previous evening was working the counter. He was delighted.

Me: "We are checking in. I have a reservation."

Him: <tapping on his keyboard> "Let me pull that up for you...OH YES! Here you are!"

Me: <dryly> "Here I am indeed."

Him: "Yes, I booked your reservation for you on the phone earlier this week."

Me: "Oh yes! You did a wonderful job seeing as we have a room and all."

Him: <peering at Mr. Tip, a mixture of awe and enchantment> "And this is your husband?"

Me: "No, it's my boyfriend" <his face fell> "Just kidding...yes, this is the lucky guy who is going to use his law enforcement discount to get us a better rate."

At this point the Tiplets were pretty much running amok in the lobby, pushing each other on the luggage cart, pushing each other in general, pushing every one of my fucking nerves..."SIT ON THE COUCH," I snapped and somehow they complied. I returned my attention to the Desk Boy.

"We are gonna need a first floor room if one's available," I sighed wearily. Then winked at him because I knew he NEEDED that to make it happen. "And one with a door separating the living area as we previously discussed."

He laughed. "None of those are finished being remodeled," he explained for the tenth time.

"Then I need one with a loud bathroom fan, if you know what I'm sayin'."

He had me covered.

Mr. Tip had not only failed to read up on my most recent shenanigans, but he also forgot his saline solution for his contacts. I bring pretty much all of the things when I travel. Soap, shampoo, makeup remover, make up, brushes and eleventy billion outfits (because I just can't predict my mood or the weather). I do not bring saline because I give zero fucks. I typically use the same solution for my contacts for days, until the flakes of dirt and mascara soak up all its effectiveness. Plus I forgot.

Mr. Tip: <listening to his Inner Squirrels, pilfering through all my shit> "Where the hell is the saline?"

Me: "I didn't bring any. Ask Rah-rah."

Rah-rah: <pointedly> "I figured YOU would have some."

Me: "So three of us wear contacts and none of us brought solution. But I have four kinds of spray in conditioner. And body butter. And sunscreen. Go ask Desk Boy if he has any."

So Mr. Tip huffed off, irritated by my packing ineptness, (thus securing no need for a separating door OR noisy bathroom fan) and went down to the front desk.

Mr. Tip: "Do you all keep any saline?"

Desk Boy: <mesmerized in the presence of such a stud to still receive admitted intercourse from his hot, young wife on the regular...so he stuttered a bit> "Um. No. Sir I'm sorry. We don't keep any saline back here."

Mr. Tip: "It's ok. I can run to the gas station."

Desk Boy: <eagerly pulling a bottle of Replenish from beneath his desk> "Well, we have some contact solution if that's helpful?"

Mr. Tip: <baffled. Did he think I wanted a fucking bag of ringers??> "Yeah, that will work, thanks man."

Mr. Tip returned triumphant. And told me the story. "SERIOUSLY, what the hell did he think I wanted it for? To flush my damn IV?"

I considered this. "No. He prolly thought you needed it for sex." He stared at me.

"Why would he think that?"

"Ohhhh, I dunno, asshat. You might wanna catch up on The Tip."

"Oh gawd," he giggled after reading my reservation debacle.

"It's the same guy?"

I nodded.

"I guess I need to go ask if he has any Astroglide down there."

"You really owe it to him, Honey. He has been very helpful."

The Case of the Missing Daisy Dukes

Mr. Tip: <digging through his pile of clean laundry> "Whatever happened to all of my cut off jean shorts?"

Me: "Well, 1990 ended and then seven years later we met and a couple years after that I threw all your shit away. Except one pair that was too small for ME when we MET. I think you wore them in middle school or some shit. I kept those so we could laugh about it without the threat of you actually wearing them."

Mr. Tip: "Why is it okay for YOU to wear cut off shorts?"

Me: "Because I have a vagina. And good legs."

Mr. Tip: "Well, I'm going to cut off some of my old wranglers."

Me: "Then people will think you also have a vagina."

Mr. Tip: <laughing> "No they won't! If I cut them short enough, the tip can peek out."

Me: "I'm pretty sure that's not going to happen."

Mr. Tip: "Whyyyyyyyy not?"

Me: "Because you do not have enough hair remaining to grow a meaningful mullet. In the event you can produce a bonafide mullet (business in the front, party in the back), you can wear all the damn 80s shorts you want. I'll even permit a cutoff football jersey and hiking boots. Because there is all fucking kinds of WIN there."

Mr. Tip: "I just want a freaking pair of jean shorts!"

Me: Fine. "I keep my tampons in a box under the sink. Help yourself, but please let me know BEFORE we run out, okay?"

Starting Off on the Right Foot

When I get a call from the school DURING school, I get slightly stressed. It's typically something innocuous (Rasslin has a nosebleed, Squirrel Master forgot how he's getting home, Rasslin forgot his glasses, Squirrel Master forgot how he's getting home, Rasslin needs his math book, Squirrel Master forgot how he's getting home...) but the "I need to have a conference with you because your son referred to another student as a koala-fucking asshat" or "Someone puked in class" call could come at any moment.

When my phone rang and I saw it was the school, I braced myself. It was one of the nice office ladies and she informed me Rasslin' was complaining about his ear hurting.

"He doesn't have a fever, but he says it really hurts. What do you want me to do?"

"Um. Kiss his cheek, smack his ass and send him back to class? Or just send him back to class."

End call.

Approximately ten minutes later the phone rang again. This time it was a very pitiful Rasslin', sniffling and crying.

Him: "Mom?"

Me: "Dude. What's wrong?"

Him: <falling all the fucking way apart> "MY EAR HURTZZZZ! SO BAD. SOOOOO BADDDDDD."

Me: "Awww, Bud, I'm sorry. You don't have an infection, I don't think. I bet you just have a stuffy nose or something. When you get home this afternoon I'll put a compress on it. Okay?"

Him: "Mom, I can't WAIT that long!"

Me: <heart slightly breaking> "By the time I could get to you now, you'd be on your way home. What if I send Mimmy (aka The Queen's

Mother) over to check on you and give you some Tylenol? That way you'll have that in your system before you get home."

Him: <still upset> "M'kay."

I hung up again and started trying to reach my mother. A few seconds later the phone rang again. This time it was the fucking snatch-maggoted office bitch who thinks she is In Charge Of All The Things. I can't stomach her. She is really short and hits me about tit level, so any time she's yapping about how I need a current BACKGROUND CHECK or immunization form or who knows what, I stare down at the top of her head and fantasize about kicking her in the taco or elbowing her in the teeth. Or both. And also she always has fucked up eyeliner. Straighten that shit out.

Me: "Hello?"

Snatch-Maggot: "I WAS JUST SPEAKING WITH RASSLIN AND HE SAID YOU WILL BE SENDING HIS GRANDMOTHER TO ADMINISTER MEDICATION?"

Me: <playing dumb> "Is that a question?"

Snatch-Maggot: <haughtily> "SHE IS NOT ALLOWED TO COME AND GIVE HIM MEDICATION. I CAN SEND HIM HOME WITH A FORM..."

Me: "Hold up. I told my son that I would send my mother to check on him. It is none of your damn business what she does with her grandson."

Snatch-Maggot: <totally persistent> "WELL, IT IS AGAINST THE LAW FOR HER TO ADMINISTER MEDICATION WITHOUT WRITTEN PERMISSION FROM A PHYSICIAN. I DIDN'T WANT HER TO COME UP HERE FOR NO REASON."

Hold the fucking phone. My shit slipped slightly, but I didn't totally lose it (we are five days in. I have to pace myself).

Me: <taking a deep, cleansing breath whilst envisioning her trollesque ass flying backwards after a well placed cunt-punt> "Listen. It may be against SCHOOL POLICY but there is NO LAW that prohibits my MOTHER from administering medication to my child.

Which she WAS NOT DOING (you nosy twat). As my son's LEGAL GUARDIAN, I can send her to the school with every NSAID in the pharmacy, have her sign his ass out, march out in the parking lot, give him one of each and then send him back to class. Mind. Your. OWN. Business."

Snatch-Maggot: <quietly> "I can send him home with a form."

Me: "I don't need a form. I need you to get bent."

So much for starting the year off peacefully.

Bird Pages

It is Football Day. These Saturday mornings are wrought with stress and frustration because my sons DO NOT UNDERSTAND THE GRAVITY OF BEING ON TIME and their father is not a morning person and also an asshole.

For my part I'm pretty much ZFG because I find it ri-fuckin-diculous that they have to be there more than an hour before the game starts. By the time everyone is in the car (Mr. Tip giving all of the fucks, me concerned only with the whereabouts of my missing sunglasses) it's time for a Valium. This morning the Squirrel Master bounded in the car with a shitload of mail.

Him: "MOM I GOT ALL THE MAILS!!"

Me: "Hot damn. I hope there is a bill for me."

Mr. Tip: <opening the driver's side door> "WHERE IS MY MOTHERFUCKING GATE BADGE?"

Me: <tentatively> "Prolly with my sunglasses."

Mr. Tip: <slamming the door and stomping off presumably to rifle through his shit in search of the badge> "GODDAMMIT. We are going to be LATE."

Me: <ever supportive> "Let me know if you run across those sunglasses!"

By this time the girls had their headphones in and had checked completely out.

Squirrel Master: "Mom?"

Me: <oh God. Here we go> "What."

Squirrel Master: "When am I going to get my bird pages?"

Me: <absently> "I don't know, Dude."

Him: "YES YOU DO. My birrrrd pages."

Me: "What is a 'bird page'?"

Him: <speaking very slowly as if I were struggling with a severe mental incapacity> "YOU. KNOW. MY. BIRD. PAGES."

Me: "YOU CAN SAY "BIRD PAGES" SEVENTEEN MORE TIMES AND I STILL WON'T KNOW WHAT IN THE HELL YOU'RE TALKING ABOUT."

Rasslin: <sensing it was time to get involved> "He means 'magazine'. The one you order Cisco's toys from."

Squirrel Master: "Yep. My Bird Pages Magazine. And also my bra pages. I never see those anymore."

Me: "Those are my Victoria Secret catalogs."

Rasslin: "Then why are they addressed to Dad?"

Me: "Because Dad wears girls underwear."

I divulged this info just as Mr. Tip jumped in the car. There was blessed silence for a moment. Then Squirrel Master spoke up.

Squirrel Master: "Dad?"

Mr. Tip: <still struggling with his personal squirrels, disorganized and pissy> "What?"

Squirrel Master: "Why do you wear girls underwears?"

Mr. Tip: <clearly confused> "I don't know what you're talking about."

This is why my children will need therapy. And also why I'm the muthafuckin Queen.

Of Everything.

Can You Smell My Swagger

My crotchfruit are excellent about getting themselves up and ready in the mornings, mostly because Rah-rah undergoes an extensive beautification process at the asscrack of dawn and makes sure her siblings are awake in time to catch the bus. Usually I join them to chat about their after school schedules that day and prohibit poor choices such as the Squirrel Master snarfing down three mixing bowls full of Froot Loops or Rasslin' wearing the same pair of muddy socks for the 3rd day in a row.

This morning I was folding laundry when Rasslin slouched by, hands stuffed in the pockets of his hoodie, precariously close to invading my psychological bubble.

“What are you doing?” I asked, riffling through a stack of eleventy-billion clean, unmatched socks answering the “Why in the HELL are you wearing the same socks AGAIN?” query for myself.

He didn't respond immediately so I glanced up. He was standing in front of me, finger hooked in his belt loop wearing a rumpled football hoodie, a pair of jeans and cowboy boots. He had accessorized this winning fashion statement with a mismatched paracord necklace and bracelet. “Is that what you're wearing to school?” I wondered.

“You don't have gym today, do you?”

“Yeah. I don't have gym. Does it look awesome?”

I smiled, “Sure!” but thought to myself “if the look you're going for is Nerdy Brokeback Mountain.”

“Do you smell that?” he wondered.

“Dude. There are two games I refuse to play. One is 'Sniff my Finger.' The other is 'What's that Smell?' Did you fart or something? And seriously, what is the deal with your necklace? "

“Dad said it was cool,” he explained.

"Son, your father wore a long, thick, herringbone chain that he picked up at a flea mall in his youth. It turned his entire neck and chest green but he rocked that shit like a street corner pimp."

At the peak of his snatch wrangling, my husband had to spray the bitches off with a hose, no doubt.

"Please do not make the mistake of allowing his misguided sense of style to influence your daily attire. Unless you like it, then rock out with your peacock out."

"I like it," he declared. "Can you smell my swagger?"

"I don't know what you're talking about," I inhaled deeply. "And I don't smell anything except cat food. Does 'swagger' mean 'fart'?"

He disappeared abruptly. When he returned I handed him a stack of his underwear and instructed him to put them away.

"Look," he demanded, procuring a stick of Old Spice deodorant entitled "SWAGGER". (What the fucking fuck?) "Podgee gave me it when we were on vacation."

"Gave it to me," I Grammar Nazied distractedly, all of Rasslin's "Danny Zuco" behavior over the course of the past week finally making sense.

"It's my SWAG, Mom!" he grinned crookedly. "The chicks dig it."

Oh Gawd. He has been going to school, putting his armpit in girls' faces and announcing he's got swagger. He is DEFINITELY his father's son. Since I can't have coffee I'm going back to bed.

It's good to be Queen.

McPerv

Friday nights are insane. I drop the boys at football practice, then pick Rah-rah up from cheerleading and rush her to tumbling--you'd THINK that shit would be the same fucking thing. But you'd be wrong. (Because like, 'oh MAH gawd we TOTALLY have a competition tomorrow and like, I REALLY need to make sure I can hit my standing back handspring on the counts and WHAT IF MY BUMP FALLS OUT? And--' fine. I'll take you.) Except for tonight her gymnastics coach had a scheduling crisis and had to cancel.

There were tears. "Mom. I can't DO IT. I'm going to totally BLOW IT tomorrow." Luckily there was a Plan B. Several of the girls on the squad have a group tumbling class on Fridays and one of them was going to miss so Rah-rah was able to fill in. Unfortunately it was 25 minutes away and well, fuck me. While we were waiting for her, I asked Velvet if she wanted a snack.

"Do you want McDonalds while we wait for that hot mess to finish her business?" I asked her.

"I guess," she responded.

"I'll get one of their yogurts."

The Starchy Arches were fairly close so we pulled in and Velvet announced she was going to wash her hands. Good plan. Because Ebola mostly. I was waiting in line (Seriously? People WAIT for this shit?) when a random guy in the line behind me struck up a conversation.

Hard-up: "It's really starting to feel like fall, huh?"

Me: <nodding> "Yeah. We just got back from the coast. I miss the warm but the leaves have been gorgeous this year."

Hard-up: "Oh yeah? That's why you're so tan then!"

Me: <Hm. Is he hitting on me? He might be fucking hitting on me. I need to remember to put my damn rings back on...> "Yeah, I did lots of basking."

Velvet returned from the restroom having taken enough time to scrub in for surgery when "it happened".

Hard-up: "So, can I buy you a cup of coffee or something?"

Me: <Holy shit. He IS hitting on me. And now my kid is here, listening in> "No thanks. My husband is working overtime so I can buy all the coffee I want. Thanks though." <grabbing our bag and my ice water to go> "Have a great night!"

As we were walking off Velvet hissed incredulously, "Was that guy HITTING ON YOU?"

"I don't think so," I shrugged uncomfortably. "He was just being nice."

She glanced back. "THEN WHY IS HE STARING AT YOUR BUTT??"

"Because my butt is awesome. Drop it."

We collected the boys, then Rah-rah who hopped in the car all sweaty and smelling like feet.

Velvet announced, "MOM GOT HIT ON AT MCDONALD'S."

Rah-rah responded instantly, without missing a beat, "Gross. Did you get me anything?"

"Some fries. How was your lesson?" I tried to change the subject.

"Fine," she chirped. "I did a roundoff with two handsprings. And got my standing back. Was he cute?"

"Was who cute?"

"Your stalker," she clarified with a mouthful of fries.

"He was cute for an old guy," Velvet declared. "He was TOTALLY staring at Mom's BUTT."

Rah-rah shrugged. "They stare at her boobs, too. All the time. Even Dad can't help himself."

"But DAD is ALLOWED," Velvet argued, indignant.

"Mom, you need to wear your rings. It lessens the Perv Factor,"

Rah-rah conceded. “Agreed.”

“And Velvet needs to take less time in the toilet.”

“Why were you in the toilet?” Rah-rah wondered. “Did you take a dump at McDonalds?”

“No, I just washed my hands and came back out to Mr. Perv trying to take Mom on a date. Dad would have been mad.”

“He prolly wouldn't,” Rah-rah countered, offhandedly. “He asked her out once too. He understands that she's hawt.”

“Could we talk about something else? Like the Ebola outbreak or ISIS or toenail fungus...I'm over the McPerv situation. Let's get the boys some pizza. They're hungry and I don't want to trash the kitchen any more than it already is.”

“Will you put on your wedding ring when we get home?” Velvet pressed.

“Absofuckingloutely. If they fit. Anxiety makes my hands swell. And if I can find them. And if I can't then I'll buy new ones for the rare occasions that I am alone long enough to get hit on by a random stranger in a fast food joint. But first, I'm stopping at the liquor store. Because we're out of wine and I need a lot of it now.”

Sex Party

At football practice, one of the moms asked if I'd gotten the invitation she sent on Facebook about her party she was hosting. She is a distributer for one of those charm companies. I will order all of the things, but parties are not my jam.

Me: "No, but Facebook hates me. And I hate parties."

Her: "This one will be FUN! You have to come."

Me: "Will there be wine?"

Her: "Duh."

Me: "You should invite my mom. She loves that shit and wants to order some anyway."

Her: "I just sent her a request!"

At this point another mom (and Tipper) pulled up so our three footballin spawn started some game of Pickup in the motherfucking parking lot.

Tipper: "Are you going to the party?"

Me: "Probably not. Because it's a party and people will be there. I think I'm sick that night. Or busy."

Tipper: "Shut the fuck up and go. It will be epic."

Me: "She's inviting my mother."

Tipper: "No. She. Is. Not!!!"

Me: "Yes huh. She just sent a request!"

Tipper: "Will your mom GO?"

Me: "Maybe. She likes parties almost as much as I do but I know she wanted to order some bracelets or something for the girls."

Tipper: "HOLD UP. THIS IS A SEX TOY PARTY!"

Me: <very confused> "What are you talking about?" <glancing back at the hostess who was busily sending my mother a request to her

upcoming Super Sextravaganza> "OMG. It's not the necklace shit? IT'S A FUCKING SEX TOY PARTY?!?!?"

Her: <distracted> "Oh, yeah. It's a romance thing. I thought maybe your mom was into it. You never know..."

Me: "DAMN IT. Did you send it?"

Her: "I don't know. I think so. Did you get yours?"

Me: "NO BUT MY PHONE ISN'T WORKING SO I CAN'T SEE MY MESSAGES!!!"

Tipper: "Oh well. At least you got something to write about on JTT."

So now I still don't have an invite and MY MOTHER hasn't mentioned any of the things to me.

I hope she has a helluva time.

Winner's Prayer

So Rasslin' and Co. suffered a heartbreaking defeat in overtime. We had those mouthy little fucks on the line, too. It sucks to get beat on one play, but shit happens. Mr. Tip had a fabulously inspirational speech afterwards that he delivered amongst the weeping young men through tears of his own.

When it was finished, Rasslin stood in the middle of a tight, circular wall composed of his teammates and led them in the winner's prayer (which if you don't know it, goes like this):

"Dear Lord, all the battles we go through in life we ask for a chance that's fair. A chance to equal our stride--a chance to do or dare. If we should win? Let it be by the code, with Faith and Honor held high. If we should lose, let us stand by the road and cheer as the winners go by. Day by day! We get better and better! Til we can't be beat! Won't. Be. Beat!!!"

I'm sure Rasslin stole that epicness from a movie or a Book of Motivational Football Shit, but he rocks it before and after every game. By the end of their chant all of the parents were sobbing, too. War torn and bedraggled, the players trooped up the stairs, hearts heavy, eyes red.

Rasslin threw himself into my arms and I whispered, "Dude, you seriously kicked ASS. I'm so proud of you!" He stared up at me, arms locked around my waist, a bit of snot glistening in the corner of his nostril and sniffed "Mom? Can we go eat at McDonalds?" I grinned back at him. "Sorry Playa. But McDonalds is for WINNERS."

I got all kinds of incredulous filthy looks from other units collecting their spawn, but last time I checked I used all my remaining fucks screaming in the end zone. He'll eat Wendy's.

And like it.

PDA - Public Display of Awesome

In a stunning display of Awesome, Mr. Tip just sauntered into a crowded restaurant at lunchtime and realized his fly was all the fucking way unzipped. He announced this only after I noticed him fidgeting and called him out for handling his meat in public.

“What are you doing??” I hissed. “People can SEE YOU.”

“I'm hanging funny,” he explained, making suspect stroking motions on the front of his jeans.

He then went on to enjoy his sandwich in a feeding frenzy that resulted in both mayonnaise and mustard spread across his shirt and globbed on the side of his nose.

Afterwards we stopped at the Home Depot where he blew a snot rocket roughly the size of my thumb out of his left nostril. Observing my disgust, he snickered “What?? I had a booger!” Really? Thanks for clearing that up, you nasty asshole.

Sorry ladies, he's all mine.

Beef Curtain

Rasslin and Mr. Tip were discussing strategy for their football game this weekend.

Rasslin: "We just need to get Heavy Beef to lead block for me and I'll break through the line and score all day long!"

Me: "Who in the hell is 'Heavy Beef'? Rasslin filled me in on the player sporting this unfortunate moniker."

Mr. Tip: <correcting> "It's 'Heavy Dee', not BEEF."

Rasslin: "No it's not."

Me: "Could we please change his nickname to 'Beef Curtain'? Because that would make me happy."

Rasslin: "What's a 'beef curtain'?"

Me: "It's a very strong offensive lineman, capable of blocking a superstar of your caliber."

Rasslin: "That's it! We are changing it to 'Beef Curtain.' I will tell him at practice tomorrow."

Mr. Tip: <completely irritated> "Goddammit. I hope you're happy."

Oh, let me assure you--I'm fucking ecstatic. :)

All hail Beef Curtain!!

Crotch Warmers

After an estrogen packed morning at a cheer competition, Mr. Tip and I raced to make it to Rasslin's final football game in his Youth career. If my train wrecked husband was any indication, I figured he would be nervous, or at least somber and focused. He greeted me with a hug and his trademark dimpled grin.

"Hey Mom!" he chirped. "Guess what?"

Me: "I'd rather not..."

Him: "My friend Beef Curtain gave me some Hot Hands to keep me warm for the game!!"

Me: "Where did you put them?"

Him: "Well, you're supposed to put them in your pocket to keep your fingers loose so you don't fumble."

Me: "I'm aware of their intended use, Son. Where the hell are YOURS??"

Him: "I PUT THEM IN MY CUP HOLDER!"

Me: <confused> "What 'cup holder'?"

Him: "You know, where you're supposed to put your CUP. To protect your BINGO."

Me: "You don't wear a Bingo Protector?"

Him: <scowling> "No. It weighs me down, Mom!!"

Oh right. My bad.

After a couple of plays I noticed my son frantically digging around inside his pants. He fished the warmers out of his crotch and ran them over to the sideline. He paused to give me a thumbs up before running back to his position.

After an epic victory he ran up to me and said "So, my junk almost burned off in the game, I'm pretty sure putting them in my cup holder was not a 'recommended use'."

"I suppose not," I responded.

"So what did you do with them?" "Oh I gave them to some girls for a souvenir."

Of course you did.

Boom.

Human Hair

Velvet will be playing Lt. Brannigan in her school's production of Guys and Dolls in a couple of weeks. (Her sister Rah-rah is going to be Adelaide, so we have heard lots of laments and Bushels and Pecks over the last few months.)

Anyway, to enhance her character and costume, The Queen's Mother bought her a moustache. Velvet's requisites were for it to be "as authentic as possible." This pre-packaged womb broom arrived over the weekend and my mom was delighted to show it to her.

"Oh wow! It looks so REAL!" Velvet breathed. Then she examined the wording which stated "Made with Human Hair" and swallowed thickly.

"What's wrong?" I wondered aloud.

"It says they made it with people hair. But it doesn't say WHAT KIND of people hair. What if it's some old man's pubes I'm about to put on my face?"

Sounds like a Date Night with your Dad.

Pregnancy and Infant Loss

When my 3rd child was a little over a year old, I discovered I was pregnant again. It was my fourth baby in four years and we would later learn Number Five was also hanging out in there. I was overwhelmed, underpaid and completely exhausted. The timing could have been better but there was no use crying over spilled baby gravy. We could handle it. We would make it work.

I started bleeding early in my second trimester and nothing could be done to save my unborn babies. As I was being wheeled into an emergency surgery to save my life, the nurse made my husband sign a waiver permitting a hysterectomy. I don't remember much, but I remember pleading with him to tell them "NO." I wanted more kids.

The loss devastated me. The doctors were able to salvage my insides so I knew we could try again but I wanted the babies that died. I thought about them every day. I spent three months in the Dark--distant, miserable, empty and alone. Then I got knocked up with my Squirrel Master.

When I saw his tiny heart beating on an ultrasound screen for the first time, an appreciation for life I never knew before emerged from the ashes of my broken heart. He was a miracle. He was mine. I fought like hell to bring him safely into this world.

Today is Pregnancy and Infant Loss Awareness Day. I know so many stories of sadness, grief and heartbreak--peoples' lives touched by the purest souls that left us too soon. I can't look at my youngest son and not be thankful for the way things worked out, but I still sometimes wonder what they would look like, who they would be.

Please take a moment today to consider the tragic dreams and promises unrealized anytime a baby dies. And the people, forever changed, who love them and think about them still.

It is Well

More than 30,000 people saw my post about Pregnancy and Infant Loss Awareness. I'd say that's doing it right. To those of you who shared your personal stories of loss, I would just like to thank you. It is incredibly brave to expose your grief and many of your comments reduced me to tears. They brought me right back to that moment...that state of being...the Dark.

It's a grief you cannot quantify and a club that no one wants to be a part of. I am humbled and honored to have provided a platform for everyone to safely express all of the feels. It is my hope that if they have not already, your hearts will heal.

My children know about the babies we lost...the siblings that might have been. Even my Littlest knows that if I'd had "Those Other Babies" he wouldn't have been born. I believe that my ability to hold and kiss this precious boy after such a declaration is the reason my soul is now whole.

Some of you wrestle with the agony every day. I hope you find peace. But things are as they should be in my world. Rah-rah got her braces off today. (Holy shit, she looks 25.) She then complained that her teeth felt slimy and looked "too white". Um, for 5k your ass is going to smile and like it.

Velvet helped her friend with a broken ankle to class. (This was an observation made as we were signing Braceless Too-White back into school.) Then she stayed after for volleyball conditioning and requested a "healthy snack" when I picked her up. She wondered aloud if french fries from McDonald's counted because they are potatoes.

Hellz yes. Wash em down with a milkshake because calcium, right??

Rasslin informed me that he looks "super buck" in his dark-wash jeans (Seriously, I thought he said 'fuck' and lost my shit) then spent the evening perfecting his very best James Dean snarl minus a cig whilst leaning against a gymnasium wall during a school function. He had an entire squadron of Rah-rahs to practice his game on. I did manage to take a photo of his buckness to share at his wedding one day. It's going to be awesome.

The Squirrel Master did his math homework all by himself. Then he told me I looked pretty tall in my boots. (Do you mean "pretty"? Or just "tall"? Yep. Fishing for compliments from my 8-year old.) Then he asked if he could borrow my Dear Cancer-Get F*cked shirt for Pink Out Day tomorrow. That would be an awesomely epic can of worms to open, but alas, I explained, that it's not an appropriate shirt for 2nd grade. So he wants to wear it under his football jersey for his game on Saturday. Agreed.

If you've got em, hug em tight.

The Post Office

Standing in the post office this morning waiting (forfuckingever) to mail out my international shirt orders, the bitch standing behind me sniffed loudly, coughed twice and cleared her throat. I turned to glance at her to see if I was risking Ebola exposure and smiled when I noticed her glaring at me.

"Your shirt is offensive," she declared.

Having forgotten I was rockin my gorgeous Dear Cancer Get F&cked jersey, it took me a moment to process the reason for this uppity snatch maggot's unfavorable opinion of my attire.

"Really?" I responded, not unkindly. "I found your nasty assed cough to be somewhat disgusting, but since I possess a modicum of class, I elected to keep my opinion to myself."

"There are CHILDREN in here!" she pressed, pursing her lips like a constipated dog's asshole.

"Pretty sure there are some fucking NOSY BITCHES here, too, but who's keeping score?"

She stood dumbfounded, mouth hanging open like she was prepped for a deep throat ball-gagging session.

"Shut your cockhole. You're drawing flies."

It was my turn next. I sauntered up to the counter, presented my packages and informed the clerk I had some items that were shipping internationally. He was laughing.

"I'm pretty sure that was the most incredible exchange I've ever seen," he whispered. "What's on the back of it?"

I turned to show him.

"Oh my gawd. That's perfect!"

I know.

I Spy

We took the kids on an overnight road trip. The ride home always sucks but this one was compounded by pulling a horse trailer over a bumpy road and having a gassy husband. My nerves were pretty much shot.

Then the kids started with the "Stop touching me" shit that made me want to throw open the door and hurl myself on the freeway. I suggested a game. They chose "I Spy."

After a few rounds, Velvet "spied with her little eye something gray."

Rasslin shouted "JUSTIN BIEBER!!"

Rah-rah asked "How is he GRAY??"

Rasslin mumbled, "Oh, I thought you said 'gay'."

Awesome.

Rasslin's Pubes

Rasslin (age 8): "Mom? Where do you get pubes?"

Me: "Um, Oh my gawd, why are you asking me shit like this at 6 in the morning?"

Him: "Because I need information. Do you get them at a store or something?"

Me: "WHY do you need this information right NOW? Wait til your Dad gets home. You can ask him."

Him: "'ll just ask Grandma. She'll probably know. I saw them at her church anyway."

Me: <beyond intrigued> "Yeah? WHERE did you see pubes at Grandma's church?"

Him: <convinced I'm fucking with him and completely exasperated> "YOU KNOW MOM. THOSE BENCH THINGS WE SIT ON WHILE THAT GUY ON STAGE TALKS FOREVER."

Me: "You mean PEWS."

Him: "Yes. That's what I said. Pubes."

Me: "Son, without going into much detail now, it's important that you note the correct pronunciation of this item you seek. You are interested in 'PEE-YOUS'. Not 'PEE-YOUBES'."

Him: "Why? What's a pube?"

Velvet: <wandering in to brush her hair, bursting into giggles> "It's BUTT HAIR. Why is he asking you about butt hair, Mom?"

Rasslin: "IT IS NOT. Grandma TOLD me what it was called."

Velvet: "You talked to Grandma about PUBES?"

I'm admittedly delighted by this prospect. Soooooo, I let it ride. Now I need to remember to remind him to call his grandmother this afternoon :)

Adopt-a-Grandma at CVS

Rah-rah and I are sick. Hoping to rule out the Ebola, I dragged her kicking and wailing to the doctor with Velvet as my accomplice. (Mooooooommmm, I DON'T WANNA GO TO THE DOCTOR I'M <cough, gag, hack, hack> FINE!!).

Get your ass in the truck.

The doctor's office was, per usual, a steaming pile of bullshit. We do not have strep, we do not have the flu, we do not have anything diagnosable, but she gave us a prescription for inhalers and something to help with all of the coughing.

I drove to the pharmacy and when we walked in we were greeted by the sight of a plump little random crotchfruit wandering around with a huge box on his head. Fearing a fever-induced hallucination, I whispered to Velvet, "What the hell is up with that walking box?"

She giggled and confirmed my suspicions--it was indeed a fat kid with a box completely covering his head and the top half of his body. He seemed to belong to the woman working the front counter, or perhaps he was homeless and shopping for new digs. I couldn't spare a fuck, but I also couldn't pass on the opportunity to make a funny. "I wonder if that's a leftover door buster from yesterday...Turd in a Box?" Rah-rah snickered, the first emotion I've seen in days.

So I went back and gathered my necessary items and promptly forgot about the Box Headed Vagina Trophy. I had to wait for fucking Methuselah to collect her monthly meds and check her blood pressure. She had approximately eleventy-billion questions for the pharmacist and DAMMIT hurry up I feel like shit and want to go home.

Eventually we were checked out and ready to go, so I took a shortcut through the booze aisle (which would have been cheaper and more effective than the $100 worth of shit from the apothecary) only to meet back up with Methuselah leaning heavily on her cane and limping slowly to the exit. Which is when the box filled with random fat kid burst open, accompanied by some kind of horrifying strangulated noise.

It scared the piss out of me, and nearly knocked the old bitch on her ass. The presumed owner of the little shit found this development amusing. I did not, because the surprise induced a coughing fit that ultimately required a panty switch for me and a defibrillator for my ancient co-shopper. I accidentally stomped on the cackling fuck nugget's hand who immediately wailed, "OWWWW MY FINGERS!!"

It wasn't malicious or purposeful, but I wasn't sorry at all. I shot a scathing glare at the counter cunt who rushed to his aid, then took pity on Methuselah, helped her to her vehicle and mumbled to my ailing daughter that he was lucky it wasn't his fucking head. "Mom, you're funny when you're sick, too!" she chirped, toting the old woman's bag for her. Methuselah looked at me. "Your children are beautiful and polite," she smiled. "Nothing like the rude little bastard in that goddamn box."

This is how I adopted a new grandmother at CVS.

Boom.

"I Mathed It"

The Squirrel Master, deeply immersed in his homework, asked, "Mom? Is fifteen plus seventeen plus ten equal to forty-two?"

Browning meat at the stove all I could hear was popping grease, "MOM" and a shitload of numbers. "I don't know, Son," I responded, wondering where the fuck Mr. Tip was. "You have to add them all together."

"I did!" he exclaimed, producing his worksheet.

"How did you do that?" I wondered, trying to drain the meat and add that shit up at the same time. "You didn't show your work."

"I mathed it, Mom. And it's the right answer. See?" He pointed to a scrawled 42. "I show it right here."

Fuck me sideways, his answer was correct. "Did you carry your ones? Show where you did that."

He considered this. "Um, should I just draw a picture of my brain? Would that work?"

Works for me.

I'm Not Sleeping

My stupid cocksucking internet keeps dropping its connection. I called the help line. They put me on hold so I hit the speakerphone and started addressing some envelopes. Mr. Tip took the opportunity to do dirty and suggestive things with his genitalia. Kind of like a perverted clown or some shit...attempting to distract me from my irritation. It didn't work--he finally fell asleep and started snoring just as a technician came on the line.

"How may I help you this evening?" she asked perkily.

"Hold on, please," I requested, whilst hissing "stop snoring, I can't hear her!"

"I'M NOT SLEEPING!" he protested loudly, clearly startled awake. "I'M JUST SITTING HERE PLAYING WITH MY DICK!"

Oh. My. Gawd. There really is no way to gloss that over, especially when it's announced to a technician on speakerphone, so I did the only thing there was to do.

"You're on speaker, Pervie. Take that dog and pony show to the couch."

He started laughing. Which made me laugh. So hard I almost pissed. I'm pretty sure they will never fix my internet now. Not that they would've anyway...

Cheerleading Pull Cord

Rasslin and his bromance are having a fan-fucking-tastic time strolling around the tacofest here at Rah-rah Mania. The pair of them, having some vague notions of a two man brodeo in a veritable fish market were slouching in a corner eyeballing the girls doing their warm up stretches.

“I like that one,” Rasslin declared, pointing at a particularly flexible young filly doing a full split.

“I dunno,” his buddy shrugged. “Her situation looks messed up.”

I had to glance, mildly uncomfortable to be assessing a teenager's box. Which is when I noticed a cooter cork string had escaped the confines of her beaver buffer.

“Oh gawd,” I gulped, desperate to divert their attention. “What about that cute blonde over there in the green?”

“Yeah, hopefully SHE doesn't have a pull cord in her drawers,” they agreed.

This is why I fucking drink.

Bathing Like a Queen

I could have almost scripted how this Bath Thing was gonna go. Four minutes into my soak, my drink is nearly gone, and there is a banging at the door.

Squirrel Master: "Mom? What are you doing?"

Me: <goddammit> "I'm taking a bath."

Squirrel Master: "With your milkshake?"

Me: <sadly> "Yes, but it's almost gone."

Squirrel Master: "Wow! You drank it really FAST! Did you get a brain freeze?"

Me: "No. I'm fine."

Squirrel Master: "Can I come in?"

Me: "No."

Precisely three minutes passed before Rasslin stood beyond the threshold.

Rasslin: "Mom? Are you naked?"

Me: "Yes. Because I am bathing. You should try it sometime."

Rasslin: "Is your vagina covered?"

Me: "What?? No dammit! I'm taking. a. bath. I am totally naked."

Rasslin: "Well, cover it up with some bubbles or a washcloth. I want to come in."

Me: "WHAT THE HELL FOR PERVIE PERVERTON?? I am bathing, go away!"

Rasslin: "Will you make me one of those milkshakes? If you ever get done?"

Me: "Hell no."

Rasslin: "What if you don't put any alcohols in it?"

Me: "Still no. Go away."

One hundred and ten seconds later...

Squirrel Master: "MOM ARE YOU STILL TAKING THE BATH?"

Me: <defeated> "I was trying to, but I'm over it."

Squirrel Master: "Good. Can I come in?"

Me: "NO I AM BUTTHOLE NAKED. Why does EVERYONE WANT TO COME IN?!?!?"

Squirrel Master: <considering> "We just really miss you."

Rasslin: "AND WE WANT A MILKSHAKE."

Me: "Fuckin' A. Let me at least shave my damn legs and knock that off my list of Resolutions."

Rasslin: "Hurry up, Mom. You're taking forever."

They give zero fucks that the Queen desired an uninterrupted tub for a few moments of solace. They learned from the master, I suppose.

Locked Door

For some mystical reason, the locking of our bedroom door elicits some primal trigger in the brains of my spawn and they immediately commence to beating down the barrier.

They assume, I think, that we are having a party they aren't invited to...so close, yet so far.

God forbid there ever be any Sexy Time whilst they are conscious. My daughters are completely disgusted by the notion. They believe that any time their father and I are behind a closed door I'm getting The Business. I understand their neurosis. Parents should not ever copulate except to reproduce, and I am clearly much too dusty and barren to ever conceive another child. (As per The Gospel According to Rah-rah.)

This recent revelation and subsequent JTT butthurt has provoked me to do what I do best: exact psychological revenge by fucking with my Lady Tips. I'll lock the door and time how long it takes a crotchfruit to knock on it, or more commonly, nearly break the goddamn knob trying to get in.

We are leaving for Drunkapalooza in a few minutes, so I locked the bedroom door whilst Mr. Tip was pinching a loaf primarily to annoy Velvet who was watching tv in my living room.

Me: <offhandedly> "I'm locking the door."

Velvet: <disgusted> "Have fun."

Me: "Oh I will..." <Thirty-nine seconds later the door shuddered in its frame as the Squirrel Master used his lithe body as a battering ram>

Squirrel: "MOM!"

Me: "What?"

Squirrel: "DID YOU WANT TO FIX MY HAIR FOR THE PARTY?"

Me: "Sure, but I can't right now because I'm busy being Butthole Naked."

Mr. Tip: <emerging from the cloud of funk lingering in the shitter> "You're naked?? Who are you talking to?!?"

Squirrel: "MOM PUT YOUR CLOTHES ON AND FIX MY HAIR."

Rasslin: "Yeah, hurry up. My shoes are in there."

Sports Injury

As luck would have it, Rasslin finished his second match by bashing his nose on his opponent's hip whereby it erupted in a bloody geyser.

When a kid starts bleeding during all of the sportsing these days, people freak the fuck out. So the panicked parent in charge of this particular mat screeched "APPLY PRESSURE!! NOBODY MOVE, LET ME GET THE BLEACH."

Rasslin caught his breath, gave an obligatory pinch on the bridge of his nose and pretty much zero fucks whatsoever. Very quickly a bearded minion arrived with a package of "nosestoppers". He whipped out a chunk of cotton and presented it to my son to stuff up his nostril. "HERE YEE NEED THIS TA STAHP IT BLEEDIN," he informed the surrounding masses.

"I don't want that," Rasslin declared shaking his head.

"But it will stop the flow," the Blood-born Disease Nazi, slightly sweaty and out-of-sorts, explained patiently.

Rasslin glanced at me (also giving zero fucks about all of the blood but plenty that my Rumchata was gone) then stared at the large man holding his cotton wandesque plug. "I'm not putting someone else's tampon in my nose," he declared. "My mom has some in her purse. I'll use one of hers."

So Rasslin wiped his nose with a bonafide cooter cork and proceeded to finish kicking all of the ass. I totally win at parenting.

Snatch Wax Nazi

Velvet: “Mom? When are you going to make us start waxing our snatches?”

Me: <slightly taken aback> “I won't MAKE you wax ANYTHING!!”

While I feel snatch waxing is an important part of long-term twat hygiene, any pube-taming tactics you personally employ in the future are YOUR decision. Washing is the only snatch-related requirement I will impose.

Her: “Well, I don't want to have any hairs-down-there blowing in the breeze.”

Me: “Then keep your vagina covered. At all times. For the rest of your life.”

Snatch Wax Nazi: Continued

My gal-pal and I were discussing snatch waxing because duh. I am the Snatch Wax Nazi and firmly believe all women should have the pubic hair forcibly ripped from their vagina at some point in their lives.

First of all, misery loves company but also it is nice to be occasionally bare down there. Mr. Tip doesn't like hair on his plate annd I just totally crossed a line, ZFG.

Anyway, she was super bummed because the establishment she used to frequent had closed down and no one in her small town offered beaver balding. So she was wild kingdom; all granola and shit because of circumstances. She would give her Queen Victoria a swipe with a razor on occasion and still wore deodorant, but her twat was unkept.

Until she was driving through her small city streets and noticed a non-descript looking clip and curl that proudly proclaimed "NOW OFFERING BRAZILIANS".

She was elated. "JTT!" she announced, almost giddy. "The new hair place is offering brazilians!!"

"Omg," I responded, relieved and overjoyed on her behalf. "You need to go getchoo some."

So she made an appointment and arrived a little early (one must spend some quality time with one's new aesthetician before displaying one's beef curtains, you see) and nervously sashayed straight into a convention of Blue Hairs.

"What the fuck," she thought to herself, wondering which granny would be mowhawking her carpet as one lady looked up from an intricate perm setting and inquired "May I help you?"

She looked around, wondering where the spa area was. "Um, yes. I have an appointment for a Brazilian," she began.

"Oh yes," she agreed. "I think your appointment is with Ethyl. She's at lunch."

The friend sat, somewhat uncomfortably. Wondering what Ethyl would be like...if she'd been tweezing twats for long...if they would click...and where the HELL was the goddamn ROOM? and then she walked in.

"Honey, come on back!!" Ethyl boomed, having returned from her homemade chicken salad break. "Come back WHERE?" she asked, mostly curious, but starting to think she was going to be expected to expose her cooter to a room full of seniors.

"To my CHAIR," Ethyl demanded, somewhat exasperated with the friend's confusion. "For your BRAZILIAN."

Sooooo, it ended up being some kind of a treatment for her hair. Her clam is still bearded, but her tresses are smooth as fuck. I'm gonna call this one a win.

Finding Humanity

A Cheesecake Factory recently opened in our area. I've eaten at one before and the food was okay, but this sucker has been on a three to four hour wait since it opened. I have not yet had the patience to wait that length of time for a meal when there are plenty of other awesome restaurants around, but tonight I wanted a piece of cheesecake.

"Getting a cheesecake at the grocery store" was not a viable option. In fact, it steeled my resolve to brave the crowd and score a piece of cheesecake I didn't REALLY want.

So I wandered into a packed lobby (on a three hour wait) and tried to find the line for the fucking cheesecakes. It was a complete wall of humans, shuffling around, jockeying for position but my mind was set. I would not leave without cheesecake. Finally I was able to discern part of where a line might have been in the waiting To Go area and muscled my way to where some slope-headed dude began awkwardly staring at my boobs. (To clarify, it was awkward for me, not him.)

It was going to take awhile. There was nowhere to sit, and soon 3/4 Tiplets decided they wanted to 1) see what it looked like inside, 2) take a piss, 3) annoy me--so pretty soon the tiny breathing space I'd carved out for myself was torpedoed by my crochfruit. One of whom promptly farted and blamed it on Pervie.

Squirrel Master: "MOM? WHAT IS THIS PLACE FOR?"

Me: "Supposedly eating. If you're willing to starve for hours to do so."

Squirrel Master: "Oh. I thought it was a factory that makes cakes."

Rasslin: "Why are you in line? We already ate somewhere good."

Me: "Were you not present for the Cheesecake Discussion in the car?"

Rasslin: "I don't like cheesecake."

Me: "It's not for you."

Rah-rah: <joining us in a huff> "I can't find Dad in the parking lot."

Me: "He probably left us."

Rah-rah: "I'm going to stand here with you all after I pee."

Me: "Awesome. Wash your hands."

Luckily a song I knew (All of Me) came on their sound system so I was able to belt that shit out with Rasslin. Rah-rah returned and pretended not to know me. Which is when I realized the family of three was having an argument behind me.

Frazzled Mom: "SHE WON'T SAY IF SHE WANTS OREO OR COOKIE DOUGH."

Exasperated Dad: "WELL THEN PICK ONE FOR HER!"

Daughter: "AHHHHHH-AHHHHHHH."

A fairly normal scene, I'm sure, especially given the crowd and the general frustration level, but I noticed the girl had Down's syndrome. And she was having a fucking meltdown.

Frazzled Mom: "Just take her out of here. She can't even decide which one she wants."

Exasperated Dad: "But it's HER CHOICE. If she's not going to CHOOSE then she shouldn't get ANYTHING."

Daughter: <covering her face> "NOPE. AHHHHHH-AHHHHHHHH."

People were staring, whispering, one asshole was even laughing. It pissed me off. I shot Giggles a scathing look and tried to herd my spawn away to give them more room. I realized Rah-rah was gone again. I turned back to the Meltdown-in-Progress and saw my daughter squatting down next to the young lady struggling to decide what kind of cheesecake she wanted.

Rah-rah: "My favorite cheesecake here is the Cookie Dough, but I've never had the Oreo. I bet it's good, too."

Daughter: <huge grin> "YEAH!"

Rah-rah: "Do you know which one you'd like to try?"

Daughter: <face falling as she shrugged and shook her head>

Rah-rah: <extending her hand> "Well here. Let's go up and look at them. Maybe that will help."

The girl took her hand and my daughter bulldozed her way up to the glass case and showed her new friend the different choices they offered. "EXCUSE ME," she snapped at Giggles who shut his fucking twat-licker and stared at his shoes.

Frazzled Mom: "I'm really sorry. She's a mess today."

Me: "You don't have to tell me. I have two teenage girls. All. of. the. hormones."

Just then Rah-rah returned with her new friend. "Tell them what kind you decided," she prompted gently. "THE CARAMEL!" her friend declared happily. Then she and Rah-rah went on to chat about her favorite class at school and her favorite store in the mall and if she's ever seen a baby horse etc.

Frazzled Mom was still slightly frazzled and Exasperated Dad was still mostly exasperated. Entirely too many fucks flying around. We placed our order and then it was their turn.

Frazzled Mom snapped, "I FORGOT WHAT YOU DECIDED!"

Rah-rah turned around and said "Remember? The caramel?" then pointed to it in the case.

"WHAT MY FRIEND SAID!" she declared.

After everyone had ordered and we were standing around awkwardly waiting for our shit to be ready, Rah-rah's new buddy became slightly displaced and anxious. "Is it okay if we go sit down?" she asked her parents.

There were no seats. Anywhere. Frazzled Mom shrugged. Rah-rah led her buddy through the crowd and found a pair of stools at the bar. "We're just waiting for our To Go order," she explained to the waitress. They both got a water to sip on. The girl's mother kept a fretful eye on them.

"They're okay," I offered, sure I was overstepping my bounds, immensely proud of my daughter for rescuing a friend. "She doesn't have any friends," her father explained. "She's on the spectrum and it's so frustrating sometimes. No one can keep her when she's not at school, and there they make fun of her."

I glanced at my daughter, so wise and mature beyond her 13 years, grinning as she tossed her hair over her shoulder, chatting happily with this young lady who was on the brink of a nucleic meltdown moments earlier. I winked at him and stated loudly, "Most people are assholes," then stared pointedly at Giggles. (Who was still waiting. Holy shit.) "And it looks to me like she has a friend now."

Finally our order was finished. They called my name and I waved at Rah-rah that we were ready to go, texted Mr. Tip who was sleeping in the parking lot and attempted to traverse the waiting area without crushing my overpriced and long-awaited confection.

I watched my little girl stand and hug her new friend, then thank her mother for allowing her to "not be so bored waiting for my mom's stupid cheesecake."

When we got in the car, Mr. Tip sighed. "That took fucking forty-five MINUTES. What in the hell did you do in there?" Oh, I just took selfies with Squirrel and Rasslin. Sang a song. Watched Rah-rah display her humanity. But I said, "We waited for fucking cheesecake."

"I hope it was worth it," he grumbled.

I hope you read this and know that it was totally worth every second we waited, even though the cheesecake itself was kind of shitty.

Fur vs fur

Rah-rah: “Mom, what's a shaved beaver?”

Me: “Oh goody!! It's been much too long since we've had one of these chats. A shaved beaver is a prickly vagina that would be much smoother if the owner waxed it instead.”

Rah-rah: “What?? My friend has a coat that she says is made out of that!!”

Velvet: “YOUR FRIEND HAS A VAGINA COAT?”

Rah-rah: “Ew! No, I think it's animal fur.”

Me: “Yes, it is if you're talking about a coat. So scratch 'prickly vagina' and insert 'soft murdered woodland creature'.”

Good talk, girls.

Geese Wrangling

I often enjoy a trip down Memory Lane. My musings of yesteryear can be quite lengthy, (feel free to skip this one but know that Facebook will likely block every potential future post from me for the rest of all time) but flowers are made to be sniffed. So sniff we shall.

If you have been here awhile, you know I have a borderline unhealthy obsession with peacocks. Specifically owning one or two or six.

Worldly folks always ask me if I've had any previous peacock possession experience. "Well, no. But I didn't have previous PONY practical knowledge before I got my first one, or crotchfruit contact and I'd never even SEEN an African Grey before I got Cisco.

I am awesome at winging shit.

They just smirk and nod. "Did you know they scream?" So do I. It would be Beast Mode to blame that shit on a peacock.

Sometimes they will extoll the virtues of the brightly colored buzzards, proclaiming them to be vile, vicious creatures intent on the destruction of humankind. This only makes me want them more.

After all, there is no way in Hell they are meaner than a fucking goose. Or rather gaggle of geese.

I grew up in the country and our neighbors had a bunch of cool animals. Llamas that would freak out and run you over, a sheep or two and the Honking Mafia.

It started out innocently enough...three little baby geese affectionately referred to as The Darryls. And they would waddle around and honk and shit on things. Gradually their territory grew to include our side of the creek that separated the two properties. And two of the Darryls grew vaginas or whatever geese do and started shitting out eggs that hatched.

What hatched from these eggs had no semblance of domestication, rather they were tiny dragon spawns shat from the bowels of hell. What had once been "Hey! Let's ride our bikes backwards down the hill!" or "You are going to get in trouble for almost dying on that rope swing we made" became a fun game of "HOLY SHIT THE GEESE ARE OUT LET'S PLAY INSIDE." Like every damn day.

These bastards were so aberrant they would try to bite car tires (or bike tires we learned once) as they whizzed past. They were meaner than normal when they had babies.

One afternoon my brother and I were outside dicking around with our golden retriever (who had been seriously traumatized by The Darryls) when we saw him yelp and head for home. Then we heard a guttural "AAAHNKKKK".

It was the Mafia. We were about to die.

"MOOOOOVE!" I screamed at Dumbass. "THEY'RE GOING TO GET US!"

"OH YEAH!" he shouted over the honking din. "HEY I HAVE AN IDEA!"

Um, is it "run like your asshole was lit on fire?"

"NO, LET'S STEAL A BABY ONE!!"

That's fucking crazy talk. Not only is it physically impossible, but it's probably not a good plan. Even Beau is afraid and he killed a raccoon last week and a gopher yesterday. Let's just go inside. We can have cookies.

"JUST GET THE BABY STROLLER!" My sister was little at the time and rolled her little plastic crotchfruits around in a veritable stable of fine carriages.

I should have assumed a protective sisterly role and convinced him that there was other shit to do, or attempted to dissuade with a simple "Dude, this is a really bad plan," but what I actually did was screech, "KEEP THEM HERE, DISTRACT THEM--I'LL BE RIGHT BACK!"

I retrieved the perfect pram. It was a pretty big one with one of those bassinet things, I imagined it would work splendidly.

What ensued was nothing short of a cracked-out midget goat rodeo (except with geese instead of goats). Feathers and screaming and rolling the stroller to keep the big ones away long enough for him to run in and snatch a confused little one. When he had captured his prize it was my job to distract the herd with the buggy.

I failed to properly do so.

So my brother is galloping up the hill screaming at the top of his lungs clutching a stolen baby goose. The Honking Mafia is hot on his heels and I am behind the party pushing a fucking stroller, laughing so hard I got a cramp in my side and had to rest for awhile whilst it subsided.

He finally made it to the house, hurtled over the cowering dog and burst through the front door. When I joined him a few minutes later (having entered through the much safer back door) he was standing in the entryway breathing heavily and snarling

"YOU SUCK AT THE STROLLER JOB."

Then you ought not have given it to me.

"So what do we DO with this thing now?" he wondered.

"I dunno, I guess we should show Mom and Dad." Who were "napping."

I now know they were humping but at the time I thought it was perfectly normal to lock the door and "sleep" in the middle of the day. We weren't supposed to bother them except in an extreme someone-is-on-fire-or-bleeding-heavily emergency and this definitely qualified. I knocked until my Dad answered looking annoyed and disheveled. My mother was pretending to sleep.

"LOOK DAD WE CAUGHT A GOOSE!" I announced.

"WE didn't catch anything," my brother argued. "I caught it. She just laughed while I almost died. THEY CHASED ME."

Which is when our new friend started shitting like, well, a fucking goose. All over the floor and wall and angry parental unit.

"TAKE IT OUTSIDE FOR CRYING OUT LOUD!" he demanded. "It's SHITTING on ERRY-THANG."

"But I think the big gooses know we have it in here and..." I looked sadly at my innocent, trusting younger sibling. "He stole it. He has to put it back."

And he did. He has both emotional and physical scars to show for his trouble.

I adjusted my tiara and watched some TV until those pissy fuckers went to harass someone else.

I could totally wrangle a peacock.

Like a Queen.

Pool Pisser

I brought the boys to the pool for a couple of hours this morning while my Ladytips participate in their respective summer activities.

I got an awesome chair in the shade, set my shit down, lathered them up with sunscreen and sent them on their merry way.

Then I decided I had to pee. I picked up my phone and moseyed to the bathroom. When I came back, a fat bitch and her band of crotchfruit had SHOVED MY CHAIR AND POOL BAG INTO THE FUCKING SUN.

The Thundertwonk was standing there, instructing her little invading assholes to create a cabana-esque area.

"Excuse me," I began, containing my complete irritation. "My chair was under the umbrella and it accidentally got moved while I was in the bathroom."

"It wasn't an accident," she responded with a cunty smirk. "It was in my way."

"But I was here first," I replied, resisting an overwhelming urge to throat punch her and kick her in the taco.

"But you LEFT," she argued, lowering her rippling ass into a lounger.

"I went to PISS. Not to SPAIN."

She shrugged. And adjusted her ample bosom. "It's a free country," she reminded me. All of her minions stared wide-eyed.

"Fine, there is plenty of room for both of us anyway."

Then I unplugged my headphones and played Lily Allen's "Fuck You Very Much". Afroman had just started rapping about his "Colt .45" when she said

"Your music is offensive."

"You think? I guess it's a good thing it's a fucking free country then, right?"

"MY CHILDREN DON'T WANT TO HEAR THAT FILTH. I'm going to get a manager."

"You do that. As soon as you get up I'm taking my spot back."

The hefty douche-swilling twat-nugget turned a strange shade of eggplant. Then she glared pointedly at me, weighing her options. (Kick my ass or relocate her wide load.)

"Do what you gotta do," I prompted, just as Afroman was extolling the virtues of eating "that pussy like shrimp fried rice".

"Besides," I continued, "my song selection is educational. That was a SIMILE."

She lumbered to her feet. "You are extremely rude," she snapped, collecting her belongings.

"And you're a peach," I grinned, winking at her flabbergasted spawn.

"LET'S GO," she demanded, abruptly.

And they left. After animatedly complaining on the way out.

Like I give a rat's ass.

Bye Felicia...remember, don't fuck with The Queen (who occasionally displays her juvenile tendencies to make a point.)

All hail anyway.

Sharting Yum-yum sauce

Gathering our belongings to leave a fine dining establishment, Mr. Tip instructed me to "Sit here for a minute."

Me: "What the hell for? Why are we waiting?"

Him: "I've got to go to the bathroom."

Me: "Oh God. I'll just wait in the car if you're going to shit."

Him: "No, I don't have to shit, but I might have sharted. I tried to squeak one out and well...I need to go check."

Me: <stifling a giggle> "By all means."

He was gone for a few minutes and returned triumphant.

Him: "It's okay. I'm clean. It was just some ass-burning heat. I need to get home though. Like, now."

Sadly we didn't make it back to his personal throne. Now I'm sitting in a parking lot whilst he delivers a truck stop shit in an unsuspecting grocery store.

Sorry ladies. He's all mine

Bitey Bird

Me: “I know it's Summer Vacation and all, but I'm tired so we're all going to bed.”

Cisco: “SHITT!!” <shrill whistle> “Go to BED!!” <MEOWWW>

Squirrel Master: “Is one of the kittens hurt?”

Me: “No, it's Cisco being a twit.”

Teeth were brushed, a few mild protests were made but tvs were turned off and everyone headed to bed. I told them all goodnight and crawled into my big, empty, cozy nest.

Cisco: “CHIRP. CHIRRRRRP. Hey. Step up?”

Me: “DAMMIT. No one put That Bird to bed.”

Rasslin: <appearing as if by magic> “Did you yell for me?”

Me: “Yes. If your name is ‘Dammit’.”

Rasslin: <giggling> “What can I do for you?”

Me: “Will you see if one of the girls will feed and cover the bird?”

Rasslin: “I'll do it.”

Cisco: “STOP! SHUT THE DOOR. Now. RIGHT NOW.”

Me: <sighing> “No, you have to get him in the cage and feed him and right now he's holding court in the middle of the kitchen.”

Rasslin: “Mom. I can put him in his cage. It's not my first birdy bedtime rodeo.”

Fair enough.

So my son disappeared and I heard a small scuffle followed by an “OW CISCO DON'T BITE” and hysterical laughing emanating from the pissy parrot.

Epic shit.

A few moments passed before Rasslin stood in my door again.

“He bit me and LAUGHED,” he announced.

“I heard,” I responded dryly. “Did you get him in his cage?”

“Yes, but I almost lost a finger.”

“I told you, you've gotta be quick or have a vagina to avoid being bitten by the bastard at bedtime,” I implored.

“I just used the broom,” he shrugged.

Poor Asshole Cisco.

Swept away.

But much quieter now.

Tree Climbing

Enjoying the peace and tranquility of an overcast summer afternoon in the country, I was startled to hear a rustling and cracking sound followed by a thud and a grunt.

I glanced over to see Rasslin laying on his back in the middle of the yard. The Squirrel Master was high up in a tree clutching a branch and howling laughing.

"What the fuck?" I mumbled, starting towards him slightly panicked, wondering if this was an ambulatory emergency or simply a case of him having the wind knocked out of him. "Dude, are you okay?"

A few stories above us, my Squirrel announced "HE WAS DOING GOOD SWINGING ALL THE BRANCHES UNTIL HE JUST LET IT GO!" whilst Rasslin collected himself and attempted to stand.

"That's great, could you please come down? I haven't started drinking yet and I am fresh out of Valium. Let's not play Monkey in the Jungle anymore today."

Rasslin had commenced to brushing himself off when he glanced at me and said "Could you check my back? I think I landed in poop or something."

I inspected his clothing carefully. "I don't see any poop. Are you okay?"

"Well, I just crapped in my pants but yeah, nothing's broken."

The best news: "I've shit myself, but I'm not paralyzed."

So overall, a good day.

Clean-up's a Breeze

I always enjoy open, frank discussions with my crotchfruits and encourage them to ask me anything. Last night we were driving home when Rasslin posed the following query:

"How many humps does it take to make a baby?"

Me: <gasping> "What in the name of Allthatisholy kind of question is THAT?"

Mr. Tip: <struggling to right the vehicle he'd almost driven off the road> "WHAT THE HELL ARE YOU TALKING ABOUT?!? Why would you SAY shit like that?" (He is notsomuch for the open and frank. But he isn't JTT. Queen rules.)

Me: "Why would you ask that, Dude?"

Rasslin: "It's The Big Question going around school. Everyone wants to know but no one can get an answer."

Me: <resigned> "Fine. The answer is 'only one'. But it's gotta be a good one."

The other three kids were silent throughout this exchange, but once Rasslin's curiosity was satisfied, Velvet had a question of her own.

Velvet: "Did you make Dad have his balls dissected so he wouldn't need condoms?"

Me: <seriously? What the fresh FUCK?> "Well, condoms were never our birth control method of choice, but yes, he had them 'dissected' to keep us from having more babies."

Rasslin: <surprised> "Oh, I thought it was because he never throws away his teeth picker things and you yell at him and you REALLY wouldn't want to pick up those wrappers all the time."

Me: <dying> "What 'wrappers' are you referencing?"

Velvet: <offhandedly> "There are condom wrappers all over the floor at [my aunt, your sister]'s house."

Me: "OHMYGAWD. In like, random areas??"

Rasslin: "Yeah like NEXT TO THEIR BED. Just like all of Dad's teeth pickers."

Me: <horrified> "Yes that's why he did it. For easier clean up."

We pulled in the driveway and I made a beeline for the booze.

"It's cute that you're so open with the kids, Honey," my husband smirked, walking up behind me.

"I'd rather them hear the truth from us than made up shit from their friends," I reasoned, praying the vodka would work quickly.

He leaned over, pushed my hair back and kissed me on the cheek. "I love you," he said solemnly.

Which is when Rah-rah stomped through the kitchen and demanded we "relocate our Humpfest to the bedroom".

I was torn between explaining the difference betwixt a Humpfest and a peck, but decided I needed a break anyway.

Mr. Tip had to leave for work unfortunately, but Mr. Vodka had no plans for the evening.

All fucking hail.

Deep Thoughts

My Squirrel Master is notorious for coming up with little known math facts. Today he announced that his age was always the same as Rah-rah's grade.

Squirrel Master: "So when I turned ONE, Rah-rah started the first grade."

Me: <head hurting from the maths> "I guess you're right! That's pretty cool."

Him: "Yeah, next year she will be in 9th grade and I'll be 9. This year she's 8th grade and I'm eight. It's been that way the whole time she's been in school!"

Me: <attempting to engage in these deep mathematical thoughts whilst slyly hiding my counting fingers under the table> "So what happens when she graduates high school? Will you turn college?"

Him: <staring at me> "No Mom. I'll turn thirteen. And the magic will be ended."

Me: <sniffling> "I don't want the magic to end. That makes me sad."

Him: "Well hopefully there will be NEW magic, but that magic will be over. Maybe I can think of a new one."

Me: "Yeah, let's get her graduated first."

Him: "Yeah, and I have to congratulate the third grade. That one's gonna be hard. I have to learn 'divide by'."

Me: <shrugging> "I still don't know that one sometimes."

Him: <dubiously> "And you're a grown up?"

Me: "Sort of. I mean, I guess. Is 'divide by' a requisite for true aging?"

Him: "No. Looking old is how you know you're grown up."

Me: "So I'm a grown up?"

Him: <sighing> "Yeah. More than me!"

Me: “I love you.”

Him: <blushing> “We were talking about math and how old we are. Why do you have to bring up that stuff?”

Me: “Because no matter how big you get or old you are, I never want you to forget that I love you.”

Him: “You tell me all the time.”

Me: “So if I'm not here to tell you, you'll remember. Okay?”

Him: “Yeah. Wait. Where are you going? Are you talking about dying?”

Me: “Holy shitballs, NO. Unless, well...let's just think of some more things to math, okay? While I have some wine and you attempt to cling to any smidge of youthful innocence you possibly can.”

Him: “Maybe later. I have to get my stuff ready for school tomorrow.”

As he walked away looking much older than his eight years, he stopped and said “Hey Mom? I love you too, okay?”

I definitely have mixed drinks about feelings. Pour me another.

Boom.

Snatch Master

Squirrel Master: "Mom? Did you know you look really very pretty today?"

Me: <suspiciously glancing down at my shitty tank top and covertly sniffing an armpit> "Hmmm. I haven't showered for in a while but I finally elected to hide my greasy hair under a hat...I was thinking I look kind of gross."

Squirrel Master: "Yeah. Well that hat IS awesome on you."

Me: <curious> "So what do you want?"

Him: "Nothing. Well. Do you want to hear me make a fart sound with my leg?"

Me: "Sure. But only cuz you said I'm pretty."

Him: "Girls like when you say that. I don't know why."

Me: <over the melodic and very convincing leg-farting> "It doesn't matter why. They really like you to open doors and shit for them too."

Him: <shrugging> "Yeah. I know."

And so it is written that the Squirrel Master shall one day become the Master of Snatch. Like a boss.

All hail.

Doctor McCreamy

Rah-rah and Rasslin needed their physicals for the upcoming sportsing that will be happening. I took them to a clinic where they went from station to station instead of having everything assessed by a single physician.

It was pretty much awesome. Especially since the orthopedic guy was SUPERfuckinghawt.

Rasslin strode in first, the doc quickly ascertained that he didn't know his right from his left but he passed him anyway, assuring me with a wink that he would likely acquire those vital skills in middle school.

Rah-rah was next. Because I had told her at the beginning of the process that an examination of her vaginal area would occur at some point, she was on the verge of a meltdown. When he asked her to lay down she covered her eyes and moaned.

"Does something hurt?" he asked, ridiculously cute in his doctorly concern.

"Noooooooooo," she whimpered, sidling over to the table. "I REALLY don't want to do this."

"Lay on the table?" he wondered. "It's fairly steady, I'll help you up."

She hesitated. Reconsidered her future as a cheerleader. Died a little. Backed towards the door and looked at me with desperation.

Which is when I decided my passport to Hell was well stamped where this event was concerned, so I let her off the hook. "He's just going to check your joints, not your snatch."

The doc covered his mouth. "I'm just going to check your leg where you broke it," he promised her. "I'm not THAT kind of doctor, though it is very important that we have those things attended to, it won't be today, on this table. I promise."

She acquiesced but shot me a filthy look. "Mom, I was REALLY STRESSED," she hissed.

The doctor stifled a laugh at our exchange, finished checking her over then stood her up and sent her off, grinning, to the next station.

"She's tall for a freshman," he observed as she flounced off, relieved to know she would not endure any cooter critique.

I smiled dryly. "I think she gets that from me."

"Looks to me like she gets a lot of things from you, including that amazing smile."

Oh gawd. Someone took it too far and now I am engaged in a flirtatious exchange with Dr. McCreamyourjeans. And I'm not wearing my fucking rings. Shitshitshit. On the one hand, I'm flattered, on the other, I'm extremely married.

Whilst debating how to unembarassingly extricate myself from the situation, Velvet poked her head in the door. "WHAT ARE YOU DOING?" she demanded. "They are like, TOTALLY FINISHED UP down there. And I'm hungry. Where is DAD?"

"Somewhere being completely sexy I'm sure. He just can't help himself," I replied pointedly for the good Doc's benefit. It was the best I could do.

Velvet rolled her eyes. "Mom, you're so weird."

I'm also having a damn hot flash.

We're out of here.

AND the physicals are done.

All hail.

Peacock Fight

Dad just called to inform me he'd seen two male peacocks fighting over a girl one at some farm he was at. They were "showing their asses and flying at one another" and he was sorry I missed it.

I told him I was sorry he didn't grab one up as a special birthday gift to himself and me.

"You're crazier than hell," he responded at this notion. "It's the Peacock Revolution. They were screaming and dive bombing each other and shit."

Me: "That's why you need to pick the one getting his ass kicked."

Him: "AND DO WHAT WITH HIM?"

Me: "I dunno. Throw a tarp over him and wrap him up."

Him: <thoughtfully> "I don't think it would work."

Me: "Come on, Dad. Back when we were kids, Doofus and I caught a shitload of geese with just a baby stroller and a dream."

Him: "You all were idiots. I'd like to see you tackle these massive bastards with just a fucking stroller and a dream. You'd need a dart gun and a death wish I think."

Me: "Has getting older destroyed your sense of adventure?"

Him: "Yes. I think it has. I'm not much for peacock wrangling."

Me: "You're never too old to try new things. Maybe you should wait for the babies and we'll swipe a few of those."

Him: "Now you're talking..."

Grasshopper

My cell phone rang. It was a random number from another state which I am not in the habit of answering, but I thought there was an off chance a Tiplet had borrowed a friend's phone, so I answered.

Me: "Hello?"

Random-male-voice-not-belonging-to-a-Tiplet: "Hey."

There was a pause and I was fairly certain that it was the wrong number, but he continued: "So what are you doing?"

Me: "Well, I just got done changing the sheets that one of my kids sharted on and I'm listening to the other one barf right now. What have you been up to?"

Random caller: "Ummm, is this Bianca?"

Cisco: "STOP. Hello? Go to BED."

Me: "No, but that is a FABULOUS name. Does Bianca have children that may be puking or shitting themselves? Cuz if not, I might be willing to trade her."

Cisco: <screaming> "SHIT! SHUTTHEDOOR." <fart. Farrrrrrrt>

Him: <uncertainly> "I don't know if she has kids. I've been texting her and she told me to call her and it took me forever to work up the nerve to call."

Me: "Ahhh, so Bianca is a potential love interest. Why are you sweatin' it? Is she incredibly hawt? Out of your league?"

Him: "Yeah, she's pretty hot. Who is that screaming in the background?"

Me: "My bird. He's an asshole."

Cisco: "Hey. Hello? Step up?" <WHISTLEEEEEEE>

Me: "Well, call her. Stop dicking around on the phone with me and call her. Start with this story."

Him: <laughing> “Your bird is awesome.”

Me: <reiterating> “He's an asshole. So are you going to call her?”

Cisco: “GO TO BED. MACIEEEEE. ROSA? Hey. Heyyyyyy.”

Him: “Dialing the wrong number straight out the gate is probably a sign I shouldn't.”

Me: “You not calling her after listening to me discuss my shitting, barfing children and enduring the antics of my asshole parrot is a sign you have no balls. Check your pants and the number and call her ass. Let me know how it goes.”

Him: “Yes ma'am.”

About 20 minutes later I got a text: “She said ‘yes’. I'm taking her bowling on Friday night.”

Congrats, my random grasshopper. I wish you and Bianca every happiness at the bowling alley.

Royal Whiskerbiscuit

The Royal Baby was born this morning. I've always been (like most of the world) in awe of the wonder that is Princess Kate, but my lady garden shrank in horror when I saw her gloriously coiffed postpartum ass tottering in heels on the steps of the maternity wing a mere ten hours after shitting out a watermelon.

I realize the wife of the heir to the throne has a team of stylists and 'people' and they earned their money today. Standing in front of the hoards of admirers, new princess sleeping peacefully in her arms, Kate looked like she'd spent a few hours at the spa, not like she just evicted an 8 plus pound crotchfruit from the Royal Whiskerbiscuit.

When I was twelve hours post vaginal expulsion, it took a great deal of negotiating with God Himself just to waddle across the room and hover above the toilet. Walking hurt, laughing hurt, pissing hurt and I vowed never to shit ever again. And I looked more pregnant when I left than when I got there.

Anyway, I hope that under the Duchess's lovely Jenny Packham was a frozen maxi pad, a wad of tucks and a not-yet-worn-off episiotomy anesthetic. And I hope she crawled out of that Range Rover and straight into a pair of ratty yoga pants and huge comfy bed where she could snuggle with her sweet babies.

All hail the new princess!

Seeded

Squirrel Master: “Mom?”

Me: <bracing myself> “Yeah, Bud.”

SM: “How did you know you were going to have me?”

Me: <relieved sigh, he's asked much worse> “Well, I got really sick and had to go to the hospital. The doctors there told me.”

Him: “Really sick? What happened?”

Me: “I was doing something with one of the other kids and I got really dizzy and passed out.”

Him: “YOU PAST OUT? How did you get to the hospital?”

Me: <oh Gawd> “I called your Podge to come and take me to the doctor because Dad was working. And when he got there I was throwing up and not making much sense. So he called an ambulance.”

Him: “I RODE IN AN AMBULANCE WHEN I WAS IN YOUR BELLY?”

Me: “Yeah. And once when you were three weeks old, too. You had a cold called ‘RSV’ and they couldn't get you to breathe.”

SM: “Well, I don't remember either ride.”

Me: “I remember enough for both of us.”

SM: “So did they turn on the lights?”

Me: “Yep. Both times. But I don't remember much about that part. I remember puking though.”

SM: “So when you got to the hospital the doctor looked to see if Dad had planted my Seed?”

Me: “They checked a bunch of stuff out because I was so sick, but at some point they decided to do a Seed check and that's how we found out we were having you.”

SM: <concerned> “How did they check for the Seed?”

Me: “It was no big deal--just a blood test.”

SM: "I WAS IN YOUR BLOOD??"

<Well shit. Here we are again: me kind of wanting to crawl in a hole and him not even close to letting up on the inquisition.>

Me: "No. You were where you were supposed to be, but the doctor checked for a hormone in my blood to tell if I was pregnant."

Him: "Why didn't they just ask Dad?"

Me: "Ask Dad what?"

Him: "If he gave you a Seed?"

<kill me now>

Me: "I dunno. I guess they thought he might not remember that far back."

Him: <considering> "Were you happy?"

I took his hand and looked at him. "Buddy, I was so very happy."

Him: "Even though you were sick and Dad forgot to tell you about the Seed?"

Me: "Even though I was sick. Every day. For nine months. You were worth every second of it."

Him: "Is that why you didn't have more kids? Because you were sick?"

Me: "No, I didn't have more kids because you were so perfect I knew our family was complete."

Him: "So Dad kept the rest of his seeds to himself."

Me: "Close enough. Do you want me to make you a peanut butter sandwich?"

Him: "No thanks. I had a Pop-tard."

Me: "I love you."

Him: "I know. Can I play on your iPad?"

Yes. Hell yes. For the whole rest of the day. I think I will strike the word "seed" from my vocabulary for the rest of all time.

Grills and Dogs

We had an awesome dog when we were kids. He was a golden retriever named Beaucephus and his self appointed lot in life was to keep us from killing ourselves.

He dragged us off of Big Wheels when we rode them too fast down the steep incline that was our driveway. He intercepted the sleds when we tried to pilot them into the frozen creek (if you got any air at all there was a fine chance you could skip that cold bastard altogether but more often than not we ended up sitting in the frigid waters). He killed raccoons and gophers and even a pair of coyotes once. There WAS one time he gave up chasing us on the intertubes my dad was dragging through the snow with the tractor, electing instead to bark like a crazed asshole (until my mom figured out what was going on and put a swift stop to all of the awesome) but for the most part, he took his job seriously.

We were on our own with the fucking geese. Beau was good at shielding us from most threats, but he wasn't dumb.

Anyway, one afternoon my Dad was doing something in the barn when my brother came up and asked me if I'd watch Beau while he went and rode his bike.

“Um, NO,” I replied, busying myself tidying the tack room. “He doesn't need WATCHING.”

“Yes HUH,” my brother replied. “I'm going to ride my bike and he'll follow me.”

My father, looking up from the board he fooling around with wondered aloud, “What in the hell is wrong with him following you? Are you going somewhere you're not supposed to GO? Don't ride the damn bike in the creek again.”

The Nerd shrugged and took off, Beau following loyally and happily behind.

A few minutes passed. I turned the horse I was brushing out in her pasture and Dad finished up whatever the he was doing.

Which is when we heard it:

A crash, followed by a bang, followed by the most ungodly clatter and racket even in the history of clattery rackets. This ruckus was accompanied by a series of desperate howls and yelps.

We ran to the driveway just in time to see good ole Beau disappear over the hilltop pulling Dad's brand-spanking-new-state-of-the-art Weber like some sort of deranged steed hauling a glorious chariot of shrieking metal.

"Oh mah GAWD," Dad stammered, a tear forming in his eye. "He tied the DOG to MY FUCKING GRILL!"

"Beau! Come!" I shouted, helpfully, hoping to entice the traumatized animal to at least stop running.

"DON'T TELL HIM TO COME!" he snapped, fucks flying everywhere. "HE'S GOING TO DRAG IT MORE!"

Well, he doesn't know the command "STOP" and besides, maybe uphill will be less destructive than downhill, I reasoned, INTERNALLY. These days I would suggest such stellar logic out loud, but back then I did have a slight sense of self-preservation in the face of such anger.

So I just nodded wisely and said, "Dad. You just gotta worry about the things you can control."

The details are kind of blurry after that. I know for sure I spent the summer honing my "Cooking Hot Dogs Over An Open Flame" skills because we sure as shit weren't getting another grill.

The Nerd learned to tie Beau to the porch when he wished to go on unaccompanied adventures.

The dog learned nothing--he was just doing his duty, after all.

And we placed another mile marker on Memory Lane.

Swagmaster

Tonight was Rah-rah's birthday bash. Her entire 8th grade class was invited (and a goodly portion showed up) for some old-fashioned bonfire fun.

I thought it would be a great idea to sharpie the cups with the names of the attendees so I could a) learn them and b) so no one drank out of anyone else's shit.

I asked one unfamiliar man-child what he wished to be called and he responded "The Swagmaster General."

I smiled and pointed to my cup. "Cool. I'm the Queen."

He nodded. "Yeah. I noticed your tiara. I didn't know if you were a princess or what. But I knew you were special."

The fucking Swagmaster indeed.

Anyway, there was smore making and fire jumping and stallion riding and singing...I'm going to call it a win. Even though I smell like smoke and I'm not drunk.

Yet.

Taste Bugs

Still sleeping soundly approximately fifteen minutes before my alarm went off, I was jolted awake by a whispered "Mom? Hey Mom!! Are you awake?"

It was the Squirrel Master, pulling on his tongue.

I struggled to focus, saw him yanking on his mouth then buried my head in my pillow.

Me: <muffled> "What are you DOINGGGGG?"

Squirrel: <completely squirreled> "Can you see my tongue? Why can I taste stuff on the TOP of it and not the BOTTOM? Because of my taste bugs? Are those the holes on top of it?"

Me: "Where the hell are my glasses?"

Squirrel: <holding my specs in one hand and his tongue in the other> "Can you SEE the bugs?"

Me: "They are BUDS not BUGS."

Squirrel: <understanding> "Like your friends? Friends that make you taste things? Even the ones that make you taste yuck like puke?"

Me: <sighing> "Ask the library for a book."

Squirrel: "I need to turn in my Area 51 book. It has aliens there."

Me: "Well, it's a testing facility for the Air Force. Some people think they found aliens or something. Did you read it?"

Squirrel: "Yep and Area 51 is where they landed."

Me: "I don't really know. I should probably read your book. And drink copious amounts of coffee."

Squirrel: <considering> "Mom? What Area are we in? Do we get aliens too?"

Me: "Do you know what they call people who drink booze before 7am?"

Squirrel: <ciphering on it> "I'm not sure. I can ask my teacher."

Me: "You do that. And I'll remember to gift her with a fifth of something special before school's out."

Squirrel: "Did you know scientists made a machine that measures gold bars?"

Me: "Omg. Did you know that the bus will be here in ten minutes?"

Squirrel: "I should prolly get dressed then! And I still need to poop."

I need a nap.

Laundry

Rasslin and I were folding laundry when he said, “This load coming out of the dryer is almost all towels.”

Me: “How do you know?”

Cisco: “NO! GO TO BED!”

Rasslin: “Because I started the wash and I put mostly towels in there.”

Cisco: “Stop. Stop that right now! Hey. Heyyyyyy. Macie? Rosa!!RRRRROOOOOSSSSAAAA!!”

Me: <confused> “But I did all of the towels yesterday.”

Rasslin: “Well. I washed them again.”

Me: “WHY? Why do the towels need to be double washed??”

Cisco: “Shit. SHITTTTT.” <scream>

Rasslin: “Well, we ran out of toilet paper and it's just not SAFE to use any towels after they have been laying around.”

Me: <dreading the answer> “Where were they lying around?”

Cisco: “No! Shut the door!” RARRRRRRRRRR.

Rasslin: “In the bathroom. And while I would never, SOME PEOPLE WIPE THEIR BUTTS ON THEM.”

Me: “WHY DON'T “SOME PEOPLE” USE A FUCKING PAPER TOWEL?”

Rasslin: <shrugging> “Maybe they're afraid the toilet will get clogged.”

Me: “I'm totally grossed out.”

Cisco: <floofing his feathers> “Whatttt?”

Rasslin: <knowledgeably> “Then you don't even want to KNOW about the SOCKS.”

Teach Me to Art

My Squirrel Master just informed me he got a new art teacher because his old teacher "respired".

Him: "She told us her name is Miss______ and that she has a cat and it's her only family."

Me: "Oh, so she's not married."

Him: "You can't marry a cat, Mom, and that is her ONLY family."

Me: "What's her cat's name?"

Him: "I don't know. She told us but I already forgot."

Me: "Hmmm. Well is she pretty?"

Him: <scowling> "NO. She's a TEACHER."

Me: "Is she a PRETTY teacher?"

Him: <borderline pissy> "Her job is to be NICE and teach me how to ART. It doesn't matter if she's PRETTY."

Which is when Rasslin rolled in and said "Oh are you talking about the new art chick? She's straight up HAWT. In an artsy way."

And she's married to a cat.

JTTeachings

Rah-rah decided she needed some chocolate before we headed home so we stopped at a small confectionary on the outskirts of town. She was in the store for a few minutes and emerged, glowing, with a bag full of fudge.

Sliding into the car she simpered, “Mom, the guy working in there was SO NICE! He said 'Hello, Gorgeous,” when I walked in, let me try samples of allofthethings and THEN gave me a DISCOUNT!”

“So basically what you're telling me is the horny teenage manspawn working the fudge counter has no clue that you're total jailbait and was hitting on you,” I clarified.

“He wasn't that cute, but he was SO NICE,” she acknowledged, oblivious to the underage reference.

Just then, Mr. Tip, having purchased a discount pair of the ugliest shoes in the history of shoes, slid into the driver's seat.

“Yeah, 'nice' guys want ass too,” I imparted wisely.”

Welcome to a JTTeaching moment, Grasshopper.

“I want you to go back in the store and tell Nice Horndog that his fudge is amazing and you'd like another piece to go. Explain you only have $5 and see what he does. Do not forget to show him your $5,000 smile a LOT. See what happens.”

“What the fuck is going on?” Mr. Tip wondered, having jammed his purchase in the cargo area. “Did she not already get her damn candy? Why is she going back in?”

“She needs more, I guess,” I shushed him.

Moments later my daughter re-emerged with a bag full of rich, heavenly fudge along with the original $5 I gave her.

“MOM HE GAVE ME A TON FOR FREE AND SAID IT WAS A SAMPLE AND TO COME BACK AND SEE HIM!” She was delighted.

My husband was horrified. “You sent her back in the store to FLIRT for FREE SHIT?”

"No. I sent her back into the store so that she could get a feel for her feminine powers in a safe environment. It was a teachable moment. Plus I got us some fudge." I corrected him, soothingly.

"Oh my GOD," he shuddered.

"The blatant abuse of feminine wiles is not mastered by trial and error after all, it's a fucking LEGACY??

"She's only THIRTEEN. That kid in there is probably 18. You should not be TEACHING HER THIS SHIT."

I rolled my eyes and turned to Rah-rah. "Sometime when Dad isn't with us, I'll show you how to convince boys to load your purchases in the vehicle because they are 'too cumbersome' for you to manage. Always use your given assets and remember kindness is your most valuable one."

She nodded. Mr. Tip, having recovered slightly from his coronary event was still disgruntled. "She is too young for this shit."

"I think maybe you're just too old," I disagreed. "You're never too young to learn basic requisites to be Queen."

He pressed his lips together, annoyed.

"Crap," I continued, changing the subject. "I'm not sure where I put my iPad. Do you remember packing it?"

"I think it's in the back. Do you need it right now?"

"Maybe, I'll just grab it really quick. Hopefully it's on top."

"No, I'll get it," he declared. "You will make a mess of all the shit I just packed."

While my husband was digging for electronics I turned to my daughter and winked. "See? It's easy."

She was impressed. "Mom, you are like a really clever magician."

More like a brain ninja. And you definitely aren't old enough to know how I maintain that particular level of control, but crying on demand is a fine starting point. Now pass me my tiara. It's good to be Queen.

Travel Plans

My crotchfruit are on Spring Break this week so we are going up to the mountains to celebrate Rasslin's 11th birthday.

I hadn't really told the kids about it because such a revelation would result in the Squirrel Master asking "how much longer til we leave?" a minimum of eleventy billion times before we ACTUALLY leave--it makes me nuts.

Today Rasslin said "Mom, Velvet says we are going to a cabin this week."

"Oh really?" I replied. "Since when is Velvet in charge of our itinerary?"

"I dunno," he admitted. "I didn't even believe her."

"Why not?" I wondered.

"Ever since that one time when I was four and she gave me a glass of pee and told me it was apple juice AND I DRANK IT AND PUKED, I don't trust a word that comes out of her mouth," he declared.

"I don't blame you. Carry on."

Since we are heading out of town for a few days I gave my crotchfruit a short list of items to pack and let them have at it.

My requirements were a pair of shorts, a pair of jeans, a few shirts and underwear.

Rasslin packed exactly one pair of underwear and assured me that between those and the drawers he was wearing he would weather the week just fine.

He was overridden. (Put some fucking skivvies in your bag and we'll pretend this convo never happened.)

Anyway, everyone had their shit pretty much together and stacked in the living room to go out to the car.

Which is when Princess Rah-rah rolled in with her large suitcase and duffel bag. The baggage of her choosing easily carries all of the shit Mr. Tip and I use throughout the course of a two week stay on the coast. Sans duffel.

Me: "What the hell is that?"

Her: "All of the stuff that was on your packing list."

Me: "And also your entire damn wardrobe? We are going for three days. You are not taking all that shit."

Her: "BUT MOM I NEED IT ALL!!"

Me: <unzipping the stuffed satchel and discovering an abundance of apparel> "This is insane. In what universe do you imagine you might wear all of this?"

She had it all...three pairs of jeans, hoodies, bras, a swimsuit, shampoo, uggs, flip flops...allofthethings.

Me: "Where are your hiking shoes?"

Her: "I can wear my Sperry's!!"

Me: "OMG NO. You'll break your damn ankle and THEN WHAT? Did you fit your crutches in that mess?"

Her: <glaring> "Hiking is dumb."

Me: "Put this shit away. You can bring whatever you can pack in the duffel."

Her: "THAT'S NOT FAIR! I might need all of these things!"

Me: "Life's not fair sometimes. And just so as you know, Rasslin may need to borrow some of your panties."

Her: <butthurt> "Well he needs to pack them in HIS bag. I don't have ROOM ANYMORE."

After the lecture about only bringing necessities, I forgot the fucking Rumchata.

Karma's a skanky 'ho.

Graffiti giggles

Driving home from gymnastics tonight, the Squirrel Master made the following casual declaration:

"Someone drew a ballsack on the bathroom wall at school."

Awesome news.

Me: "How do you know it was a ballsack??"

Him: "Because it had short little lines for where the hair goes."

Me: "So it was a HAIRY ballsack?"

Him: "Yeah, I guess!!"

Me: "Well how do you know it was a ballsack and not a little cactus or something?"

Him: "Because it was attached to a big ole WIENER. You could even see the bingus HOLE, Mom."

Me: "Oh gawd. Did you draw it??" <resisting the urge to joke about cacti and pricks>

Him: <emphatically> "NO. Remember that one time I put a bingus on my boy drawing in Sunday School and you like, FREAKED OUT?"

Me: "I will never forget the day of the 'Anatomically Correct' church gaffe. But you didn't do ANOTHER ONE in the toilet stall did you?"

Him: <logically> "No. It was just a bingus and prickly balls. All alone. If I was drawing it I would put it on a guy--where it belongs."

Me: "Don't draw dicks on the walls, okay?"

Him: "I won't. Or ballsacks."

Me: "Or vaginas or boobs. Or the f-word."

Him: "I promise."

Afterword

Rah-rah

Fourteen years ago I began a journey, the parameters of which had been alluded to, but not fully disclosed. While all of the cliches and corny things a new mother hears are true, perspectives change when you hold your baby in your arms for the first time.

The most remarkable thing about motherhood is finding pieces of your soul you never knew existed, pieces you could never again live without.

My first labor was an easy one. I had a great epidural that wore off in time for me to push a few times whereby I was presented with a squirming, screaming lady baby.

We did not have an ultrasound to determine gender, so I was expecting a boy one. I wanted a girl so desperately I had CONVINCED myself I'd have a man-child so that my disappointment wouldn't preclude me from being a decent mother before I even began.

Then she was there and I was so overwhelmed I didn't know what to do. I cried. I held her briefly, counted her tiny fingers and toes, then passed her off to her daddy.

It is hard for me to articulate my feelings for my children and how they have evolved over the years. My sons and daughters are not a reflection of me, responsible for my failed dreams and desires. They aren't a second chance for me to get shit right. More and more, I find myself falling in love with them for the people they are becoming.

I have so many hopes for my girl. I hope she one day knows true love and true peace. I hope she learns what friendship is. I hope she discerns the petty from the precious. I hope she laughs. I hope she sees her own beauty without compliments or mirrors.

I hope she eventually forgives me for perceived injustices and I pray that one day, she will look at her own child and realize that I have loved her more than anything.

Velvet

Today is my younger daughter's birthday. She was born after a difficult pregnancy, and when I wasn't vomiting or begging my cervix to stay closed (with the aid of Magnesium Sulfate aka the Piss of Satan) I was worried that there was no way I could love another kid as much as I loved my first.

She emerged after a brief labor (so fast in fact that my damn epidural didn't have time to work) ready to take on the world and prove me wrong. My daughter is wise beyond her years and quickly taught me that love knows no bounds. She is slow to judge and quick to forgive. She is a friend to those suffering and gives to those in need.

She loves animals and possesses a rare strength and beauty in her ability to communicate with them. She can ride the hell out of a horse. She inspires me every day. She is smart and funny and kind. She is most comfortable in her boots and jeans and when she smiles, she lights up a room.

She is standing on the brink of womanhood, endless possibilities before her, ready to kick ass and take names.

So please join me in wishing my younger daughter a very happy birthday, and many more ☺ XOXO

Rasslin

My third pregnancy was mostly unremarkable, except to say that it followed so closely behind my first and second crotchfruits that I pretended I wasn't knocked up until I couldn't see my feet anymore.

If I'm being honest, I was probably suffering from a double whammy dose of postpartum depression already when the Rasslin seed was planted. It was a Dark Time and I sucked at being pregnant even when I desperately yearned to bring forth new life from my lady garden.

I was PISSED when I learned I was having a boy. I mean, if I was going to shit out three kids in less than three years at least they should be the same gender so they could share clothes.

Rasslin was born on April Fool's Day. Everyone was in the room at 12:34 pm...two doctors, a gang of nurses, Mr. Tip, my parents, random strangers...I didn't give a shit. (Well, at least not until I started pushing. Then that's a different story.)

When he was born the room was ghastly silent. And in a split second, that moment of quiet when the breath leaves your body and your lungs struggle to fill...I gave approximately eleventy billion fucks.

"WHY IS MY BABY NOT CRYING??" I panicked, having been suddenly abandoned in the wake of the new arrival.

"He's okay," the doctor (the same guy that said I'd prolly be fine waiting six months to start back on the Pill) assured me, whilst crocheting my vagina back together. "They are cleaning him up."

"BUT I CAN'T HEAR HIM," I gulped, convinced my baby was dying and no one dared admit the truth.

Then Mr. Tip laid him in my arms. And my tiny son simply looked past my tear-filled eyes into the depths of my soul. I couldn't hear him when he was born because he didn't cry. He was just taking it all in.

Before that moment, I knew what love was. I'd been in love, I'd given birth, I knew loss, I understood sacrifice. But it had never gut-punched me like that. My whole life had led up to this moment of unexpected joy.

I was blessed on this day eleven years ago with a gift I didn't know I wanted. That I had no clue I needed. That changed me forever.

My son is still teaching me things I didn't know I needed to learn. The seventh digit of pi. How to make a rocket with a box of matches. Stitches really don't hurt THAT bad and some shit is worth a trip to the hospital. All girls have cooties--except me. Winning is important. Losing isn't the end of the world.

Everything is an adventure if you look at the world through the eyes of a boy.

Please join me in wishing Rasslin a happy 11th birthday.

I think I've got something in my eye.

Squirrel Master

The delivery of my youngest son was tough. It was bloody. It was drugless. The pregnancy was worse.

I was so sick my doctor ordered the placement of a picc line to keep me from dying from all the puking.

My Squirrel Master was my fourth child in five and a half years, but his arrival followed a pregnancy that didn't have a happy ending. I fought hard for him for 38.5 weeks, visiting a high risk obstetrician weekly, monitoring his growth while carefully managing a host of pregnancy related health issues.

He was born with a gross knot in his cord after a stalled labor, loads of pitocin and (like I said) no pain management. It fucking sucked.

Then he emerged wailing--the doctor laid him on my deflated stomach and he was beautiful and my husband (with tears in his eyes) said "I'm so proud of you. You're amazing. And I'm pretty sure you burst my eardrum with all the screaming."

Yeah? If you want to see busted, take a look at my vagina after they're done sewing it up, Asshat.

Today is my youngest child's eighth birthday. He completed our family and teaches me every single day that the biggest challenges offer the greatest rewards. He experiences the world differently than I do, and provides insights that I am infinitely lucky to experience with him.

So we are going to ride along the coast in a topless Pony with some great friends and amazing family. We're going to eat whatever the hell we want. We're going to lay in the sand and build sandcastles.

We'll probably pee in the ocean.

We will laugh.

And for a moment, acknowledge how blessed we are as we remember that one time The Littlest Vagina Nugget Fell Out of Mom's Butt. Happy birthday, Master of Squirrels <3

About the Author

KC Meadows, aka Her Royal Highness (HRH) or Just the Tip, hosts a Facebook page regaling more than 30,000 loyal followers with the humor and angst of her daily life as a mother of four hilarious and precocious children. She wrote this book at the behest of many devoted Tippers and her husband who implored no fewer than eleventy billion times, "Honey, you really SHOULD write a book!"

All hail